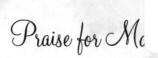

Praise for Ma...

"Diva of desire Regena Thomashauer teaches women how to celebrate their passions, indulge their appetites, and adore their lives."

—*Chicago Tribune*

"She looks like Ava Gardner, thinks like Marie Curie, and makes Dorothy Parker seem tongue-tied. And needless to say, she has fabulous sex. How can you argue with that?"

—*The New York Times*

"At Mama Gena's School of Womanly Arts, you check your shame and self-denial at the door, and learn to claim what you have always desired."

—*Elle*

"Mama Gena advocates a life where ecstasy, fun, and happiness are the rule, not the exception. . . . Her combination of composure and charisma makes her the most alluring woman I've ever met."

—*Sunday Express* (London)

"Pleasure is absolutely of the essence. . . . Regena Thomashauer [is] a testament to the principles of taking control of men and 'pussifying the world.'"

—*The Independent* (London)

ALSO BY REGENA THOMASHAUER

Mama Gena's School of Womanly Arts

Mama Gena's Owner's and Operator's Guide to Men

Mama Gena's Marriage Manual

Regena Thomashauer

SIMON & SCHUSTER PAPERBACKS

New York London Toronto Sydney

SIMON & SCHUSTER PAPERBACKS
Rockefeller Center
1230 Avenue of the Americas
New York, NY 10020

Copyright © 2004 by Regena Thomashauer
All rights reserved,
including the right of reproduction
in whole or in part in any form.

First Simon & Schuster paperback edition 2005

SIMON & SCHUSTER PAPERBACKS and colophon are registered trademarks
of Simon & Schuster, Inc.

"Comment" from *Dorothy Parker: Complete Poems* by Dorothy Parker. Copyright © by the
National Association for the Advancement of Colored People. Used by permission of
Penguin, a division of Penguin Group (USA) Inc.

Permission to reprint "Something Wonderful" by Richard Rodgers and
Oscar Hammerstein II Copyright © 1951 by Richard Rodgers and Oscar Hammerstein II.
Copyright renewed. Williamson Music owner of publication and allied rights
throughout the world. International copyright secured.
All Rights Reserved. Used by permission.

For information about special discounts for bulk purchases,
please contact Simon & Schuster Special Sales at 1-800-456-6798
or business@simonandschuster.com.

Designed by Helene Berinsky

Manufactured in the United States of America

2   4   6   8   10   9   7   5   3   1

The Library of Congress has cataloged the hardcover edition as follows:
Thomashauer, Regena.
Mama Gena's marriage manual / Regena Thomashauer.
p. cm.
1. Marriage. I. Title.
HQ734.T446   2004
646.7'8—dc22   2004045432

ISBN 0-7432-6109-7
0-7432-6110-0 (pbk)

*This book is dedicated to all romantic fools
who would do anything for love, even get married.*

Author's Note

The stories about people told in this book reflect feelings or situations which many of us have experienced in our own lives. While the essence of the stories is real, many are composites and, in most cases, names of individuals and other characteristics have been changed.

Contents

Mama Gena's Marriage Manual

Introduction

Oh, life is a glorious cycle of song,
A medley of extemporanea;
And love is a thing that can never go wrong;
And I am Marie of Roumania.

—Dorothy Parker

Darlings!!!! Have no fear, Mama Gena is here!

Well, darlings, she's back. The irrepressible, outrageous, fabulously irreverent Mama Gena is here to break open the seal on the secret to a fabulous marriage. Marriage, today, is about as relevant an institution as the National Rifle Association. Mama wants to renovate, to revive, to revitalize! To tear down the existing structure and build something new, something fabulous, something that will accommodate everything a woman is, and everything a woman wants. If Mama can make room, within every marriage, for the fulfillment of every single woman on this planet, we will have a glorious foundation from which to build passion, friendship, intimacy, and a flourishing family life for the entire world.

Congratulations on your marriage. You found yourself a kick-ass man, you owned, you operated, you dragged him back to your cave . . . and now, what do you do? You don't know what the hell to do, do you?

Wives are driving themselves into the ground in oh so many ways. Remember Party Girl Patty, in her hot leather miniskirt, who used to go wild and dance on the bar every Tuesday? Since the wedding, Patty doesn't even go out to party with her girlfriends anymore. Or what about Party Girl Sally, who is the talk of the town, criticized by everyone in her church group because she's married, with a child, and she still goes out in a miniskirt with her girlfriends every Tuesday? What's a party girl to do? And what about Fat Nancy who seems to eat a whole cheesecake by herself every time her husband has another affair? Or sweet Rachel who is inconsolable now that her kids are in college and she is all alone with the big, boring lug? Or disillusioned Susan who had this fantasy of living in a big house in the suburbs and being a full-time mom, and now that she's there, she is so isolated and lonely, with her husband working fifteen hours a day, that she can barely function? Or Constance, whose hairdresser is seeing far more of her than her husband ever did? Or Grace, who dropped out of school twenty years ago, when she became pregnant, never got the degree in nursing she always wanted, and now she is too scared to go back? Or Brenda, who never misses a chance to put her husband down in front of everyone? Mama, can we do better than this?

Is it possible to create something new, something fun, something real, something true that contains and encourages the hot, sexy, vibrant spirit of a woman? Do our *Sex and the City* days have to end? Can we be responsible, and have a blast as we love our husbands and raise our children? Can we keep the hot in our throb? Can we be flirtatious, outrageous, joyous, and still change diapers, go to the office, and have a hot hunk of manhood in our bed every night?

Marriage is misunderstood. That's why so many of them fail. We live in a world right now where over half of marriages end in divorce, and of those that survive, how many are actually happy? OK, OK, you may say, happiness was never the point. Putting food on the table, a roof over their heads, and raising children, that is the point. Ain't it so, word up. The institution of marriage was created for the purpose of the survival of the human species. And therein lies the problem. In this wealthy, abundant world, we no longer need marriage to survive. Women can support themselves very well, thank you, in the world today, and make enough money to live on their own. One-third of all babies born are born out of wedlock, so apparently you don't need wedlock to feed yourself, clothe yourself, or make babies. Seems we have all figured that one out. So what exactly is marriage for? Has it not become extinct, like a relic hanging from the ceiling in the Natural History Museum?

Are you ready? Mama's gonna tell you, but you may not be able to hear. You may even disagree. But hang with me on this one. In fact, don't agree with me about what a marriage is for. Just let this viewpoint float right alongside your viewpoint.

Ready?

Fun.

Marriage is for fun. It is to make our lives more fun than they would be without marriage.

But isn't *fun* so . . . frivolous, Mama? So shallow and unimportant? Our culture guides us to feel that way. But let's look from another perspective. Don't you love the people you have fun with? Don't you want to be with them? Don't you look forward with enthusiasm and spirit to activities that are fun? For instance, on the first sunny day of summer, you jump out of bed, pack up the car, and race to the beach. Or when you get your hands on a fantastic book, you stay up all night reading it. Why? It's fun.

Fun has restorative, youth-giving powers. That's the beauty of fun. It is attractive. When you serve fun, it pays big dividends. You can solve problems with fun, be creative with fun, create intimacy, closeness, sacredness. Rarely can you do any of those things with force or obligation. Everyone knows the fun has been sucked right out of marriage and replaced with obligation, but many people are doing it anyway, and then blaming each other, or themselves, when it does not turn out to be the solution to all their problems.

Which is why marriage is in trouble right now.

But marriage has two really big things going for it:

1. Gay people want to do it. Why is this a good thing? Because as soon as gay people move into a bad neighborhood, the property values start going up.

2. Mama Gena is here to do a massive excavation and restoration. In other words, darlings, relax, we've got you covered. All you need is an open mind.

I want to hand you the keys to the Queendom of marriage—you know, that place where your husband treats you like an absolute Goddess, and you would be lost without him.

"Where is that place, Mama?" you ask.

I'll show you.

As Goddess is my witness, I am going to hack my way through the brambles of our cultural limitations, our piss-poor education, our lack of imagination, and haul your ass there, kicking and screaming.

Welcome to the world of *Mama Gena's Marriage Manual*. I am going to shock you, encourage you, and fling open unexplored highways toward your desire. I am going to persuade you to chart very different courses, ancient and modern pathways, toward a marriage that sustains and supports your pleasure, your creative unfolding, and your burgeoning desire. A marriage in which your joy is the highest value to you and your partner. A marriage in which he lives to serve you, and his job is to make sure there is a smile on your face. A marriage in which you are married first to your pleasure, your desire. A marriage that fuels and feeds and refreshes, rather than drains and creates hopelessness and compromise. Basically, I want you to marry a woman (yourself) and him to marry a woman (you). If I can get you both to use *you* rather than *him* as the basis for your combined happiness, I have a shot at making sure you both are happy.

The life-support system of a marriage is fun, not suffering. Mama's going to seduce you into using your good times as a compass to navigate the hills and valleys of your married life. This is a world that excludes compromise and includes all that you desire. Why? Because you have no idea how good marriage can get. And I want to shake you awake to your potential in partnership. Don't you think you deserve it?

I was on the phone recently with a young woman from *Elle* magazine who was interviewing me for an article on sex and marriage. She was thirty-two years old and about to move in with her boyfriend of one year, with whom she was very much in love. Working on this article had begun to make her very nervous about marriage. "Mama," she asked me, "do you think that marriages are destined to fail? That things get less fun or less sexy over time when you're together? I have so much fun just with myself, I can't imagine that it won't be even more fun once I marry this man that I love." It was such a breath of fresh air and springtime for Yo Mama to hear a young woman who actually enjoyed her own company, who found herself to be fascinating, interesting, and enchanting, all by herself. I said, "Jo, if we can keep you loving yourself with that degree of enthusiasm, there is no possible way that your marriage will be anything other than a lifetime exploration of heaven."

Once we get this wonderful rapport going between you and your fine self, we are going to explore how to use your man and train your man in a way that leads to true partnership.

*Y*ou may not know this know this yet, but you have signed yourself up for the adventure of a lifetime. As a married woman, your potential for world-class fun, lust, love, intimacy, friendship, and exploration has never been greater. You have a partner by your side! Someone to experience the world with! You have a confidant, a loyal fan who can see you through to your dreams when your spirits are flagging. Someone to celebrate with, to cuddle you when you want consolation, to ravish you when you want sensual fulfillment, to diaper your babies when you are otherwise engaged, and to buy you things you wouldn't have thought of on your own. My darlings, a partner is the most fun tool you can have in your toolbox! If you want fun, he will amplify it. You got a problem? He wants to solve it. He can get to a point where he knows what you want before you even ask for it. Downright indispensable, that's what a man is.

Now, don't get me wrong, you and I both know that you are a succulent thing on your own. A man simply broadens your reach, expands your pleasure, and opens your doors. I do not want to talk you into a husband if you do not have one. I think life alone is divine. I just want to talk you into having fun with him if you've got him. And show you how to make really wonderful use of him, since he's already there, taking up space on your couch.

I think men, husbands, are the most underused commodities that a woman has. I'm going to show you how to tap that keg, girlfriends, and suck every juicy drop out of that man! Men love love love love to give of themselves to the women in their lives. Like the legend of King Arthur and the Knights of the Round Table, men want to be used in service to our dreams and desires. But I suspect that most of you do not know a dot about how to use your husband to serve you. So many key items were left out of our education. *Ways to use your husband in order to really have fun with him* was one of them. Money was another, and forget about sex. But I know you. You are clever. When someone gives you directions that make sense, you are willing to take the ride. How else would you have gotten to the bookstore this morning, darlings? How else would you have baked your first cupcakes, gotten your first job, or programmed your cell? Hell, Mama just spent twenty minutes with tech support on the phone resetting the power settings of her iBook. If Mama can do that, *you* can find a way to use your husband for your pleasure. This book is here as a vehicle for you to reinvent your marriage as a source of celebration instead of an energy drain.

I see so many women who get absolutely sucked dry by the Institution. They have spent much of their lives planning their wedding and looking for their prince, just as their mothers did before them. Now add a full-time job to all their expectations of themselves, and you have a generation of women who are positively fried. They are supposed to keep beautiful homes, prepare healthy meals, spend quality time with their children, bring home a paycheck, and manage their own careers while emotionally supporting and encouraging their husbands to be all that they can be, and delivering great, regular sex. And the horror of it all is that we think we can do this. The pressure is so enormous that it makes me want to curl up with my blankie and twirl my hair.

I don't know about you, but I spent my twenties darting around, doing whatever I could to hide so no one would even think about marrying me. Marriage scared me. I hadn't seen too many good ones, and I surely did not want to get myself stuck in the same knot-hole. From my high and almighty perspective, women who were married looked disappointed, or worse, they looked like fish out of water, hooked and struggling on the line. There were simply no good role models out there. I liked Jackie O's style, but life did not look so good there with Jack. It looked even worse with Ari, although she did get herself a private island. But how much fun is it to be a trophy wife? I'd rather turn tricks than marry for money. At least you get variety. And no pretense of happiness. I think pretense is the most exhausting thing in the world. Don't wear me out by making me pretend to be happy.

So many of the married people I knew in my town were miserable. Maybe miserable is overstating it, because I think that many of these couples were unaware of their low-level discomfort. I mean, if you are breathing, how can you *not* notice when your husband is having an affair? One way, and one way only. When you are gasping for breath yourself, you don't notice too much of what is going on around you. Take, for example, my neighbor Lucy. One day, after thirty years of marriage, her husband just up and vanished. Cleared out all his possessions, and his bank account, and blew out of town. Lucy was devastated. I could never understand why exactly, because Harry was no picnic. He was a real pain in the ass actually, and he was never really nice to anyone. I thought she was way better off without him. But she had become so accustomed to the lack of attention and ongoing hostility that she was lost without it.

I can still remember that retching feeling in the pit of my stomach in my twenties as I was asked, when are you planning to find a man, settle down? I was not interested doing *anything* that *everyone* expected me to do so desperately. I left home and went to a city where I did not know anyone. I had three different jobs so no one would get to know me too well. I took countless classes on evenings and weekends so my free dating time was nonexistent. I broke up with my spectacular boyfriend after seven years so no one, especially him, would get the wrong idea. I went on dating hiatus. I was an actress, so I busied myself by suffering for my art. The point is, I filled my days with so many things—activities, volunteer work, work work—that there was no possible way I could be perceived by myself or others to be on the marriage track. I was buying myself some time and perspective to figure the whole thing out. I was not about to put a satin-covered foot on the white carpet, ever, unless I could design a fun way to do it. I watched, I observed, I learned, and, most important, I experimented. In this book, I am going to share with you the results of my own personal research and the experiences of hundreds of women who carry themselves over my threshold each year.

Thirteen years ago, my husband, Bruce, and I started a company called Relationship Technologies. We taught classes for single people and couples with the goal of delivering to them the tools for creating great relationships. We wanted to experiment ourselves—working together and creating a relationship that started well and got better and better over a lifetime. Our theory was that no matter what sort of dysfunctional past or insufficient education one has had, each of us is capable of creating a great relationship with ourselves, and with partners, once some basic behavioral skills have been learned.

After a few years, I realized there was something I wanted to say to women, specifically, about relationships. I noticed that when a woman was happy with her life, her relationship was usually happy, too, and she felt in control of her destiny. And when a woman was unhappy, she was driven desperately to search for happiness in her relationship, where, suddenly, it did not exist. I resolved to show women how to find that joy within themselves, to awaken them to the incandescent joy that they were born with, and to help them create relationships that are in service to their own pleasure, rather than in service to others. Because when a woman is getting everything she wants, everyone else's life improves, too.

I created a forum called Mama Gena's School of Womanly Arts, a school devoted to the study of pleasure. The women who read my books and participate in my classes are called "Sister Goddesses." Why? Because it is my conviction that all women are sisters and that each of us possesses at least a drop of the divine within us, if not a whole lot more. Women feel that divinity most deliciously when they devote themselves to the pursuit of pleasure and the study of the Womanly Arts (those skills that, when practiced, allow us to use the power of pleasure to have our way with the world). They find that their outlook on life improves dramatically. Rather than spending all of their time in the trenches, problem solving, caretaking, and working their fingers to the bone, they are capable of reaching their goals by investigating their desires and playing with pleasure. This new perspective actually allows women to get what they want faster and with a lot more fun. When people spend their lives addressing problems, investigating their pasts, and looking at what's missing from their lives, they do not necessarily find happiness. Rather, they find that their problems have expanded. When women pursue pleasure, they discover more pleasure and experience true exhilaration.

Our courses are designed to enhance, celebrate, and inspire us to choose fun and to step into our power. You will own and enjoy your sense of pleasure, joy, sensuality, and greediness. Mama's intent is to enhance and expand the voice of women by fanning the flames of their desires, which opens the doors of fun and pleasure for everyone.

In Mama's view, a woman is the keeper of the flame of desire in a relationship. It is key that we, as women, recognize our power, our part, and our potential as the fire keepers. If you feed the flame, it glows brightly. If you blow it out, it's over. He can become your able-bodied assistant, bringing you fuel for the fire, or he can bring on cold buckets of water to help you douse it. Ultimately, it's your fire and it'll burn if you want it to.

This book is in service to desire. It is for women at any stage of relationship—whether you have been together four months or forty years. I will be disabusing you of the notion that the controls of your relationship are housed in your partner's lap. As long as we think we are not in control, we are victims of love. As soon as we see that we are in control, we can begin to explore our pleasure in partnership. Most people never take the opportunity to explore their pleasure because they are so deeply tangled in the state of victimhood that passes for relationship in our culture. Look around you right now. How many of your friends and family are in relationships that you look at and think, Wow, that looks like so much fun! I want a relationship just like that! They are so cute and sexy and laugh so much and get along so well! Don't look at people who have just started dating. I want you to look at life in the trenches of relationship—two, five, ten, twenty years down the line. How many people have got it going on? I see many partnerships in which both men and women tacitly agree, in some way, to turn off essential parts of themselves in order to keep the relationship alive. I don't want that for you. I don't want that for anyone.

Mama's going to move your marriage to higher ground. The first step is to awaken you from the coma called the Good Wife Syndrome. That is the state of suspended animation in which you do everything you think *he* wants, and you give up the things you are passionate about in order to prioritize *him*. You put yourself on a shelf somewhere in order to be a *good wife*. This altered state stifles a lot of great women and kills a lot of great relationships. So Mama's here to administer the antidote. One of the ways to ensure you never have a relapse is by gathering together a group of Sister Goddess girlfriends who share a similar goal—they all want to create great relationships with their men. Your Sister Goddess girlfriends will be there to make sure that you stop complaining and start pursuing pleasure instead. It takes a village to train a man, and you will be choosing your own village to take your marriage even higher than you could on your own.

I am going to teach you how to dedicate yourself to your joy with some simple exercises that will strengthen your stamina. Mama will teach you how to *train* your husband. This will require you giving up your whining, your complaining, and your anger. What the hell, that trio is so worn-out and moth-eaten, you will be well rid of it.

There is no room for victims in man training. Your self-defeating behaviors have had their day. There is a new kid on the block—you! Which means you can finally, once and for all, get what you want. And one of the things I *know* you want is a great sex life. Married sex can be yummy. You just can't leave it to chance—practice, practice, practice. Let's see what those eight thousand nerve endings you've got are *for*. Of course, there will be obstacles. But Mama is gonna guide you through the most common obstacles that occur in relationships, including money, in-laws, children, trust, and betrayal. There is not a single obstacle that you cannot overcome as you build a marriage based on pleasure, rather than obligation. We are in this boat together, Oh Sisters mine, so let's take this ship called *Marriage* for a four-star cruise on the open seas.

After years of exhaustive research, to which Mama has donated her body and mind, time and time again, the conclusion is simple: when you go for pleasure, you get pleasure. When you go for fun, you get fun. When you go for blame and problem examination and investigation, you create a marriage filled with hostility rather than passionate friendship. And since you are reading this book, you expose yourself as a fan of marriage as a passionate friendship. It will be our little secret. . . .

Mama wants you to get it going on. First with yourself, and then bring the whole enchilada that you are into the mouth of your relationship. You can be hot, you can be spicy, you can be stuffed with a variety of ingredients, all of which will serve to give you and your partner a taste of what life in partnership with another human being has the potential to be. I want you to have a relationship, a partnership with a man that sizzles with life, lust, and love. I want you to be the envy of every married or single person you meet. I want you to create a scene everywhere you go by the joy you bring because of the love you are living. I want you to blow open your own mind with how much you allow a man to give you, to spoil you, to pamper you. I want you to get everything your greedy little heart desires, and then some. The world exists to serve you, to celebrate you, to fulfill you. I want you to be escorted to the finest seat at the banquet table and have your husband pull out your chair. Not only do you deserve it, but the happiness of the world depends upon it.

CHAPTER ONE

The Good Wife Syndrome

Don't compromise yourself. You are all you've got.

—Janis Joplin

So much is invested in selling us a wedding. Since you were a kid, people teased you and told you that one day you would be married. You probably played bride as a child. Maybe you even played Mommy. Chances are, very few of you played Wife. What do you even do when you play wife? Maybe the reason you never played it is because it isn't much fun. Wives are rarely heroines in our cultural mythology. They don't get to go on a lot of cool adventures. Generally they stay at home weaving, like Penelope, while their husbands, like Ulysses, go on adventures. The single girls, like Charlie's Angels, or Xena or Laura Croft, seem to have the most fun. Seems like a conspicuous absence of fun in the job description: wife.

Most likely, you started planning your wedding when you were a little girl. But did you lie back and daydream about your marriage?

Did you imagine yourself becoming the biggest bad-assed, happiest married person in the whole wide world? I doubt it. And if you did think about that, I bet you pictured yourself smiling, with oven mitts and an apron. Or strolling ecstatically through the streets with a baby stroller. But did you ever stop to think, will making dinner every night really be much fun? Will pushing a stroller up and down the block thrill me day after day? And did you ever stop to think, exactly what does married sex look like or feel like? Did you wonder if anyone really looks forward to having sex with the same person for the next fifty years? Did you discuss any of these concerns about this *before* you walked down that aisle?

We have an epidemic of unhappiness in our culture right now. Sixty-five million people are on Prozac or other antidepressants. Half of marriages end in divorce. Of the marriages that do survive, many are sex-starved. The current remedies for all of this rampant unhappiness are useless. They are hiding the problem or even making it worse. The reason for all this depression and unhappy relationships is that women have constructed prisons for themselves by trying to keep their husbands and children and jobs on life support. You are trained—*trained* since birth—to ignore your happiness and pay attention to other cues. Trained to not indulge yourself. Trained to deprive yourself and serve others.

Let's take a look at how all this dissatisfaction plays out in the real world. When Sister Goddess Vivien married Arnie, she thought she was getting everything she had always wanted. He had a great job, so she could stop working and be a full-time wife and mother. She was thrilled with the house, thrilled with the wedding gifts, thrilled with the new neighborhood. But when he went to work that first morning, leaving her alone in a suburban development where she knew no one, and had nothing, really, to do except clean the house and make a dinner that he probably would not be home to eat with her because he worked so late, she sat down on her overstuffed new sofa and cried.

Several towns over, and crying, too, was Sister Goddess Marie. She had recently married, at age forty-one. While she loved Roberto, their whole first year together had been about desperately trying to conceive a child with scheduled sex and hormone shots. Then he lost his job, which meant they would have to leave San Francisco and return to London. Not exactly what she had in mind when she tied her knot.

A few towns to the left, and we peek in on Sister Goddess Anne. She is fifty years old and has been married for twelve years. Anne is on her fourth marriage. It is her best one yet, but she has settled into a quiet, parallel existence with her very sweet husband. She has her own friends, her own activities, her own life. He has become a piece of baggage that she handles now and then, that she has very little use for. She takes care of him, he gets room and board at her house, but she gets very little back from him.

And just across the river is Sister Goddess Kellie. Married for eight years, with a seven-year-old child, she is humming distractedly as she prepares dinner for the family, knowing she is about to go off to the "gym" for her "private training session" with her extremely personal trainer.

Sometimes we don't even realize we are in a coma. Sister Goddess

Raye has been married for twenty years and has two kids. Her husband is basically a doll, but for twenty years she has rather blindly allowed him to make all the decisions, all of their vacation choices, all of their lifestyle choices. She feels vaguely unhappy and rather comatose, but she never suspected it had anything to do with *her*. When vague unhappiness is on everyone's menu, one does not even think about explosive joy or soul-stirring passion.

Most women have no sense of the tremendous resignation and compromise they bring to a relationship. Shrinking to accommodate *him* is so culturally ingrained that it is virtually undetectable to women. The way to detect shrinkage is to notice how annoyed we feel over petty things each day. Notice how hostile you feel toward your guy. Notice shrinking enthusiasm about your own life. You have been watching this one TV station for your entire life, and now I want you to switch to a new channel.

Are you getting all this down, darlings? Are you taking notes? This is perhaps the most crucial thing I have to tell you in this book. Since you are trained to ignore your happiness, this manual exists solely to teach you how to pay attention to it. How much have you shrunk in your marriage? What exactly have you lost? Have you stopped growing? What parts of yourself have you not yet experienced or explored? Have you lost the feeling of your own potential? Do you have the same divine, expansive enthusiasm from your youth? Did you think these were things that you had to give up?

What's going on here, Goddesses? Fallen asleep at the wheel?

If we were all in a car, driving to Detroit, and found ourselves accidentally in Phoenix, what would we do? Pull into a gas station, I suspect, and ask directions. When you head down the Matrimonial Highway, it seems like there are no gas stations, or if there are, it's not polite to ask. Marriage has an overarching, silent agreement that we are not supposed to raise objections that would upset the apple cart. So instead of speaking about our unhappiness or, better still, our desires for happiness, we begin to rot from the inside, poisoning all the apples in the cart instead.

The Permission Man

There is a general agreement among women that men are oppressing them in marriage. How many times have you heard a married girlfriend say, "Oh, I can't [do that, wear that, go there, buy that] because my husband would never let me." When this gal was single, she seemed perfectly capable of doing and going and buying whatever she wanted, whenever she wanted. She did not require the services of a gatekeeper. Now that she's married, to behave as though her husband sets the rules is almost a badge of honor. Hey, even I have played this situation to my advantage. When shopping, for example, and trying on a $10,000 ring at Verdura that I cannot possibly afford, I say to the salesman, "I love it, but I have to bring my husband back to see it." Salesmen know about the husband. Actually, I once went to Bergdorf's with my husband, just to window-shop before a movie, and salespeople were *all over us*. Why? They assumed that Big Daddy was there to spoil his darling. The husband is the big kahoona. He is the permission man.

At some level, women know they are in control. We know that all we would have to do is sit down with our big lug, or slowly walk him over to our point of view, or flirt him into our frame of mind. But we're stuck in our expectation that he should have known already what we wanted. The husband is supposed to be the one who knows. A woman will get herself into a spot where her husband is doing something that offends or disadvantages her and she will act surprised, victimized, and blame him for it when actually she was the one who gave him the slave chains and said, "Shackle me!"

Sister Goddess Victoria had a first husband who was from Australia. She married him not just out of lust (they had a great sex life), but also because he needed a green card. But because of his lack of ambition and overuse of marijuana and her bank account, they divorced one year later. Her next husband, Lloyd, was a workaholic, filled with ambition, who never had time for, or interest in, sex. Victoria went from a rock to a hard place. But who was forcing her to marry these guys? Who insisted that she be shackled to a life that wouldn't fulfill her? If we lie down in traffic, is the car to blame?

Let's get down to business right away, girlfriends. If marriage is a prison, it is because *you* have made it so, *we* have made it so. And since we are the ones who erected the bars, set the locks, and upheld the restrictions, we are also going to have to be the ones to tear down those unpearly gates.

The Good Wife Syndrome

There is an insidious poison that seeps into many relationships, sometimes almost as quickly as they begin. A general malaise settles itself silently and invisibly, like carbon monoxide fumes in a garage. He begins to notice that there is something sticky or weighty in the air that he can't quite name, but it feels like pressure and he doesn't like it. She starts to withhold her thoughts, feelings, responses, and desires. She waits for cues from him about how and when and what she should speak about or what she should do. Like the horror movie *The Stepford Wives* many years ago: the woman in the relationship vaporizes and her replacement, the Good Wife, takes over. The syndrome is so subtle and stealthy that the woman herself does not really notice that she is evaporating. Her girlfriends may notice, but they're not alarmed. Her husband or fiancé senses something is amiss, but he can't quite put his finger on it. She herself feels a little odd, and yet self-righteous—as if everything she is doing is for the good of the *relationship,* dammit! As if the *relationship* was something far more important than she was. As if she was in charge of the relationship, or supposed to guard it with her life, or serve it, at the expense of herself. And the *relationship* seems to exclude *her* desires and *her* happiness. When a woman plays the Good Wife, or the Good Girlfriend, there is a cost. She is actually running an interior tab. She is not sacrificing herself for free, no no no. There is a price that she will exact for all this *Good* behavior. In exchange for her services, he must comply with her goals of commitment and responsibility. He must become the Good Husband or the Good Boyfriend. And if he doesn't read her mind and fulfill the agenda, she gets angry and resentful, and he does not quite understand why. There has been no discussion about this decision to be replaced by Married People clones. The process is just a consequence of societal expectations developed over thousands of years.

Here is a typical example of the Good Wife Syndrome. Sister Goddess Marsha had just moved to Atlanta, from Des Moines, with her new husband. She did not know anyone in Atlanta, and she spent her days working on a book she was writing and trying to fix up their new house. Since it was summer, most people were on vacation, and she was having a hard time finding friends. Every Friday she would get a call from her husband, asking her if it was okay if he went golfing with his buddies after work. Since Marsha was alone all week, she was looking forward desperately to the weekend with her husband, to seeing another human being who knew her. The first week he asked, Marsha wanted to be a good wife, so she said, "Yes, of course it's all right." And she proceeded to have a miserable night all alone. She went to a bad movie, and returned to her empty life, which was also a bad movie. Now, how much fun can you have the rest of the weekend after arranging a night like this for yourself? She was now angry at her husband and angry at herself for allowing her husband to desert her. And poor Steve had no idea that he ruined her evening and their weekend. He just wanted to chill out with a little golf.

The following Friday, Steve called Marsha again to ask about golfing after work. Now, this is where Good Wife Syndrome gets really ugly. Marsha, a strong, intelligent, beautiful woman who went through that awful experience last weekend and knew the consequences of golf on a Friday night to her mental health and well-being, said to Steve, "Of course. Go and have fun. I'll see you when you get home."

Now, darlings, what is up with that? And don't tell me it's just Marsha and *you* would never do such a thing. We all do this thing. We try to be some kind of version of a supportive spouse, some kind of inhuman, highly evolved being that does not have wants or desires, because we want to make *him* happy. But there is no such thing as a happy him until you get every drop of fun that's coming to you. And the hardest part will be overcoming your resistance to getting every drop that is coming to you.

Luckily, Marsha had a built-in rescue party, ready and waiting. She was enrolled in Mama Gena's Marriage Course. So when she got on the phone for her session with her gang of Sister Goddesses and moi, we all said, "Girl, have you *lost* your mind? Do you want to ruin another weekend of your life?" Marsha told us how much she wanted to prove to herself and her husband that she was a good wife. We all laughed like lunatics. And I invited her to put down the phone and call her husband at work on her cell, and invite him to come home that night and sink his putt on a different kind of green.

When Marsha got back to our call, she was totally shocked and delighted with herself. Her husband had not only agreed to come home, but he told her that it was never a contest. Between playing golf and pleasing her, he would always choose spending time with her and pleasing her. He said he was thrilled to get her call. He also said that she sounded different and that it was amazing to hear this sexy invitation from his conservative midwestern wife.

Now the interesting thing about this, aside from the lovely outcome, was that Marsha would never, in a million years, have attempted to seduce her husband away from his clubs on her own. Without her fabulous gang of Sister Goddess girlfriends to show her the potential she did not even know she had, she was all set to compromise her life, the life of her husband, and as a consequence, the life of her family and her community. The world does not need one more embittered, disappointed woman. We have hit quota on that. The world is hungry and thirsty and salivating for a happy woman who feels righteous about having her way. And none of us can be counted on to go for every drop of our desires on our own. We require other women who can see the extent of our gloriousness when we cannot experience it on our own. All of us, except Marsha, knew her husband could not resist her offer. And he was so happy to have a shot at being her knight in shining armor. In fact, the only way we can get a guy to be a hero is to saddle him with one big-assed, greedy woman who will use use, use, use him for her pleasure. Maybe that is what a good wife actually is—a woman who is willing to be good to herself, rather than prioritizing her husband's requests above her own desires. And the goal of this book is to get each and every one of our guys to hero status. Being married to a hero is so sexy. And there is a hero in every man. And you hold the key, with your lust. So be a really good wife. Start a new syndrome.

The Marriage Myth

There is a huge gap, a huge disconnect, between our expectation of married life and the actual reality of marriage. The myth and the truth are at odds. We tend to look at marriage as a solution, an antidote, a destination, a resolution. It is none of those things. It is a lifestyle choice and a discipline, just like being an athlete is a lifestyle choice and a discipline. Being married is an enormously gratifying way to live—a privilege, actually. But it requires a different set of skills than being a daughter, a mother, or a single woman.

Let's talk about what you thought you were getting. Some of you thought you were getting a soul mate, a companion, someone to take an interest in your deepest fears and loftiest dreams. You thought that somehow your union with this man was going to smooth all your rough spots, that he would come in and take care of you. Some of you devoted yourself to the cause called marriage, which to you meant giving up every part of previous life to follow your husband on the pathway to his dreams. You gave up your gang of girlfriends, you gave up your pottery class, and you gave up flirting with guys to concentrate on building a model marriage. Perhaps you thought that giving up your career to raise the kids would gratify all of your longings for creativity and personal achievement, and it would give you languorous evenings to spend with your husband, who was now your primary source of intimacy and companionship. You expected him to be the sole source of male gratification in your world: you used to have a lot of guy pals, but now you have your husband instead. You believed that your relationship with him would give you a sense of wholeness and fulfill you in ways you had always dreamed. Here are some examples of marriage fantasies from some of the Sister Goddesses, starting with mine:

> Like Cinderella, Princess Di, or Princess Grace Kelly, I step out of my pumpkin carriage and walk down the aisle to meet my prince. Our marriage is as cheerful and frothy as those depicted on *The Brady Bunch* or *The Partridge Family*. We laugh and frolic together. I tend the home, he brings home the bacon. Like these women, I follow my dear prince on the pathway to his dreams. I happily abandon whatever I was doing to devote myself to care of him and our household. In return he makes me exquisitely happy, bringing me flowers and making all the best choices for me and our lovely, well-behaved kids!

> I would be married in St. Patrick's Cathedral in New York with a New York City wedding reception. Home would be filled with laughter and two children. I'd have a handy husband who would take a sincere interest in the home. A husband who would manage all the finances and take care of the day-to-day cash flow. All the decisions would be made jointly. I would work outside the home. I would have a housekeeper. We would spend a lot of family time together without losing our own identities. We would play games, tell stories about the present, past, and future. We'd have an active sexual life that would support each other's fantasies. My husband would be my best friend. The mar-

riage would be one cohesive unit with lots and lots of love and communication.

I always thought that I would live in a huge old house, with lots of antique furniture and a big yard and flower gardens and a vegetable garden. Somewhere in the country, but near a city to go to restaurants and the theater. I didn't expect to have to work. I thought I'd be a really cool mom with several fantastic kids. My husband would make good money and we could afford to do pretty much whatever we wanted within reason. I'd be beautiful and fit, with fun hobbies. We'd have lots of interesting and close friends. I'd drive a nice BMW or Mercedes or Jaguar. As for decisions, I would make everyday decisions like the dinner menu and social schedule, but my husband would take care of all the big things like insurance and bills and stuff like that.

The Reality

In reality, marriage is not a destination. It is the beginning of an unfolding adventure that sometimes changes form as rapidly as a sandcastle at high tide and sometimes lies as still as a long, hot August afternoon. Each step we take, each choice we make, has enormous impact on our marriage, on our love.

The reality is, you marry a guy. He can only be a guy, not a universe of fulfillment for a woman. He was somebody's son, and his mother trained him as best she could. He did not take lessons in how to pleasure a woman. Or how to read your mind. Or how to buy a Victorian home, manage the cash flow, buy the right insurance, plan vacations, be the decision maker, create a loving environment, sing around the piano, make passionate love to you, or hire a staff to take care of you. He probably doesn't know exactly *how* to be your best friend, even though he would probably like to. He is especially upset to be such a disappointment to you. After all, he wanted to add to your happiness, not detract from it. He did not know you expected a one-man band. He's just a guy. Not a prince, not a knight, just a perfectly wonderful ordinary *guy*. But he could become a one-man band if someone taught him how.

Your guy wants to be a prince. He wants to be a hero. He has all the same qualities as Sir Lancelot and the Knights of the Round Table. He would throw his cape over a puddle for you, like Sir Walter Raleigh; write love sonnets to immortalize you, like William Shakespeare; erect a Taj Mahal in tribute to your beauty, like Shah Jehan; leave his throne for you, like the Duke of Windsor. Every guy is a big giant barrel of love, wanting to find a way to pour his loving devotion in his lady's direction. He is pure raw potential, waiting to be tapped, used, lapped up, enjoyed.

Not knowing how to love is not the same thing as not loving. Most men today haven't a clue how best to express or experience their heartfelt devotion to women. Men have no idea that what they are offering us is insufficient to the task of creating happiness in the marriage. They operate from their own perspective, their own experience, repeating what they learned from their parents' marriage. They have absolutely no idea that the information they possess is not remotely enough to create a foundation for happiness. The women who understand this can unleash the king in any man. There is a magnificent song from Rodgers and Hammerstein's musical *The King and I*. The wife of the king sings:

> *He will not always say*
> *What you would have him say,*
> *But now and then he'll do*
> *Something Wonderful.*
> *The thoughtless things he'll do, will hurt and worry you,*
> *Then all at once he'll do something wonderful.*
> *He has a thousand dreams*
> *That won't come true,*
> *You know that he believes in them*
> *And that's enough for you.*
> *You'll always go along,*
> *Defend him where he's wrong,*
> *And tell him, when he's strong,*
> *He is Wonderful.*

It is every man's dream to live to serve the woman he loves, and we release the magical elixir of *hero* in any man simply by loving him. The rewards for loving a man, for choosing to see his greatness, despite the obstacles, are enormous. He becomes a living tribute to his beloved's beauty, adoring her more than she could adore herself. And being that woman, capable of instigating your own adoration, is a remarkable and wonderful thing to be.

But the Good Wife Syndrome can make you antagonistic rather than adoring, and that's when your Sister Goddess girlfriends can provide a most effective antidote. Sometimes it takes a Sister Goddess girlfriend to assist us in coming to our senses and seeing our husband for the hero he truly is. Take, for example, Sister Goddess Roxanne and her gang.

One lazy afternoon, Mama was leading a correspondence call for the Owner's and Operator's Guide to Men course. Among the group of women who were on the phone call was Sister Goddess Roxanne. Mama was holding forth on the subject of men, and how they actually live to make women happy. Roxanne was oddly silent on the call. Finally she burst forth, her voice trembling with rage and tears. She confessed that her husband had no interest in her and did not care if she was happy or not. Roxanne and her husband had lapsed into a façade of closeness that attempted to conceal the great gulf that was dividing them. She had been married for twenty years to a big sweetie named Dan. She regarded him as a friendly nuisance with whom she cooperated in order to maintain her position as a nonworking wife and mother in upper-middle-class suburbia. She had totally stopped communicating with Dan. Roxanne was feeling nostalgic about her single days. She remembered feeling free and spontaneous and enthusiastic about her life. She felt she had been so much more interesting as a single person than she was as a married person. I asked her what kinds of activities she had done with Dan, before they were married, that she was no longer doing. She said that when they had first met, they had traveled a lot to very exotic places, which she adored. They had not traveled together in years. I asked her where she wanted to go. She said she had always wanted to see the Taj Mahal. When she said that, her voice possessed an excitement that Mama had not heard before. Sister Goddess Roxanne had buried her inner Taj Mahal by deciding it could never be, now that she was a married person.

"Do you want to get your enthusiasm back?" Mama asked.

"Yes," replied Roxanne.

"Then put down this phone right now and go find your husband. Wherever he is, whatever he is doing, ask him if you can interrupt and ask him a question. Ask him if he would be willing to take you to the Taj Mahal."

"Oh, Mama, I cannot do that! He would never, I would never!" she whined.

"Then don't blame him for the coma you find yourself in. Dan actually wants to make you happy, and you are not even allowing him to have a shot at it," said Mama. Roxanne found Dan watching TV. She asked if he would take her to the Taj Mahal one day. "Honey," he replied, "aren't you in the middle of a class? Can't we talk about this after your class?"

Roxanne returned to the phone in tears. "He refused me!" she reported. When Mama asked her to repeat the conversation, it was clear that Dan had not refused her at all. He had simply wanted more for her than she wanted for herself. He wanted her to have the full experience of the class, and then he wanted to give her his full attention to talk about the trip to the Taj Mahal. He had actually, in his own way, said yes.

When we, as women, deny and stomp on our own dreams and desires, we cannot even hear when our men want to gratify them. Dan was interested in her dream, but she was programmed to hear no, and that is what she heard. She had focused her attention on her own impenetrable wall of doubt and couldn't even hear her husband's response. He would have to have sent a scud missile to blow up her doubt and get his message through.

After the phone session was finished, Roxanne went in to see her husband. She was shocked and overwhelmed to find Dan on the Internet, researching what? The Taj Mahal, of course.

With that one square kick in the butt, Sister Goddess Roxanne threw off the GWS and allowed herself to be truly served and gratified by her husband. Not only did Dan have a shot at making her happy and demonstrating that he was indeed on her side, but Roxanne got a refreshing whiff of what it's like to live in her dreams and desires, rather than stifle them.

This book is an engraved invitation for you to climb on board and understand you are not alone, that every woman who is married confronts the same loneliness, the same challenges, and the same obstacles. Until we can identify the invisible limitations on our potential happiness, we can never make headway toward actual fulfillment. And then the trick is to very slowly draw your man into your vision, your truth, your desires. In the next chapter, we will identify what exactly a Sister Goddess wants to create in order to be responsible to her own joy, first and foremost, and then, consequently, to the joy of her relationship.

Exercise #1: The Fantasy

Write down your vision of marriage, what you grew up thinking it would be, full-throttle fantasy, complete with theme song.

What kind of house did your fantasy bride live in? What did she do with her days? How attentive was her prince? How was her sex life? Did he make all the decisions for her? And were they always wonderful and wise?

Exercise #2: The Reality

Write down how your life in relationship actually is. Do you talk about everything there is to talk about? Do you have sex as often as you thought you would? Do you look forward to seeing each other? Do you expose every aspect of yourself to him, or do you keep secrets?

Exercise #3: Video of the Week

Watch *A Price above Rubies,* with Renee Zellweger. See how cultural expectations perverted this vibrant woman's life.

Exercise #4: The Former You

Make a list of all the activities in your life before you met your current partner. Did you take swimming lessons? Did you go out with your girlfriends? Belong to the community theater? Did you go on vacation alone, or with friends? Did you read for hours in a café? Did you flirt and go out dancing?

Exercise #5: The "Are You Shrinking" Quiz

There are signs, subtle signs, obvious signs, that you are drifting away from your hot, sassy self, into your expectations of what a wife is.

(True or False) You can grade yourself!

1. As soon as you think of something you want, you cancel it in your own mind before even allowing it to register.

2. You shop for foods that he wants to eat, and you have eliminated goat cheese, sun-dried tomatoes, and calamata olives from your refrigerator because he does not like them.

3. You have not worn your miniskirts and halter tops in a long, long time.

4. You are fatter than ever.

5. You run around with low-grade anger, like a low-grade fever, constantly.

6. You start prioritizing his wishes above your own, serving what he likes for dinner, going to bed at his bedtime, turning down invitations to parties or events that he doesn't want to participate in.

CHAPTER TWO

The Sister Goddess Marriage

When three women join together, the stars come out in broad daylight.

—Telugu proverb

I call my students Sister Goddesses because, as women, we are all sisters and because I profoundly believe that each of us has a generous serving of the divine in every fiber of our being. It is women who create life. Women who inspire. Women who can bring out the hero in every ordinary man. Women who understand the language of ecstasy. Ah, what a privilege it is to be women, united by these abilities! Sometimes I feel like the most blessed thing on earth.

I also profoundly believe that a woman's divinity is directly linked to her ability to experience desire. When we experience that flooding feeling of desire, we feel most fantastically alive, most resoundingly ourselves, most flush with our own potential. Desire is the connection between ourselves and that which is greater than ourselves. There is a metaphysical power in a woman's desire. Just by wanting something, a woman's life force will attract it. Grace Kelly wanted to be a queen. So did Lisa Halaby. Diana Spencer did (before she changed her mind). Mary Baker Eddy had the desire to form her own religion. Any woman who uses birth control owes a debt of gratitude to Margaret Sanger's desire and the people she inspired. If we enjoy the majesty of Grand Central Station or the Central Park Reservoir, we can thank Jackie O. Look around you, and you'll see that women's desires have a supernatural ability to manifest themselves.

One of my own greatest dreams has been to tap what I consider to be the greatest untapped resource on the planet. I want to teach women how to fan the flames of their own desires. Six years ago, I taught my first Mama Gena's School of Womanly Arts class. The response was explosive. Since then, the school has received incredible national publicity, and the classes in New York are so popular that we now have a waiting list. My first class was twelve women, and today thousands of women from across the country and around the world have become Sister Goddesses. These women have rebuilt their lives around pleasure. In my classes they've explored every facet of their bodies and minds and learned the exquisite potential of the feelings and sensations within each one of us. And once they've focused on what they want, the incredible things that women are capable of conjuring, week after week, are astonishing. For instance, Sister Goddess Tiffany announced that she hates to do laundry. Last night she decided that laundry might actually be fun if it didn't take so so much time and effort. As if in answer to her prayer, she found a parking spot right in front of her apartment, which enabled her to load the car easily. Then, as she was taking the sheets out of the washer, a twenty-dollar bill fell out. When she went to use the drier, a five popped out. Tiffany was shocked by the power of her expressed desire to conjure some fun at the laundromat. When you invite abundance, she comes to dine at your table!

The bonds that the Sister Goddesses form among themselves are a critical part of the class. When you put a group of Sister Goddesses together, their power multiplies exponentially—it's more fun and more restorative than therapy. I am going to suggest to you all that the community of women that we create around us has greater effect on the outcome of our lives, especially our relationship lives, than does the partner we choose. If you can create a group of women whose goal is to feel glorious about themselves, have confidence in their desires, have confidence in each other, and expect the best from each other, with zero tolerance for each other's bullshit, I can deliver to you a group of women who have the power to form and sustain fantastic, flourishing partnerships, marriages, and families for a life-time. This new paradigm is something I have the privilege of living every day of my life, and I have created numerous different pods of Sister Goddess communities all over the world. They continue to keep in constant touch with one another and inspire each other's dreams and desires.

Women have always influenced each other's relationships. When I was in high school, I hung out with guys and gals, but the center of my social life was my gang of girlfriends. We all had adventures with boys, but then we would run back home and call each other, or sleep over at each other's houses and report on our experiences and desires.

We would even go on reconnaissance missions for one another. My friend Sally and I drove to the senior prom in our junior year and hid under the cars so we could watch the guys we had crushes on with their dates. Or Dawn asked me to find out if her boyfriend Sam had slept with his previous girlfriend. We worked it all out with each other, and for each other. When I got to college, I had the same system going on with a different group of girls. I watched as each of us moved through different boyfriends, experimenting sensually, going back to touch base with each other as we had more adventures. The decision to lose my virginity had as much to do with the fact that I was the only one in my set who hadn't, as it did with the degree of intimacy between my boyfriend and me.

Gale Berkowitz wrote about a landmark UCLA study suggesting that friendships between women are special. "They shape who we are and who we are yet to be. They soothe our tumultuous inner world, fill the emotional gaps in our marriage, and help us remember who we really are." This study, which is the first of its kind to focus on women, also found that getting together with a group of girlfriends can counteract the intense stress that most women feel every single day. It's all chemistry, really. We are wired differently than men. Laura Cousin Klein, Ph.D., now an assistant professor of biobehavioral health at Penn State University and one of the study's authors, found that when men experience stress, it triggers testosterone, which produces a fight-or-flight response. This was useful, thousands of years ago, when, let's say, a hunter in the wild became the *hunted*. When women are stressed, they release oxytocin, which modulates the flight-or-fight response and encourages them to herd with their own kind and tend the children. When a woman does gather with her gaggle, more oxytocin is released, which calms her further. We are wired to benefit from each other's presence and participation.

These days, at Sister Goddess Central, I have a unique community. I live and work in a brownstone in Manhattan with Bruce and Maggie. My pal Lori, who works with me as the directrix of the school, brings her one-year-old daughter to the Pussy Palace every day, and we share a wonderful babysitter named Marti who looks after both girls. Deborah, our directrix of special projects, decided to become pregnant as soon as she started to work with us and saw how much more fun it is to be a mom when you have a gang of girlfriends by your side. Her baby was born in January. We also have Kadidja, our administratrix of pleasure, who actually left San Francisco and moved to New York City to work at the Palace. She is beautiful and single, and she had the nerve to steal the affections of Mama's personal trainer, Andrew, as she conquers New York. Then we have Sita, our photographer, who interns with us, and just moved in with her adorable boyfriend, Justin. Bear in mind that the only man in this whole confluence of women is my husband, Bruce, the president. (He must have a kharmic debt from a past life. Even the cat and the dog are female.) Bruce says he would have it no other way.

This whole community of women is there for each other in every sense of the word. When it's Mama's birthday, Lori will remind Bruce to do a little shopping. When Lori had her baby, we not only gave her a shower but found her aimlessly wandering the streets after a stressful few days with her newborn, and gave her a place to go, stuff to distract her, and a shoulder for a good cry. In fact, with all these women taking turns holding that baby, it's a miracle she ever learned to walk. Kadidja was able to move seamlessly to a new city with instant girlfriends, an instant community, and an instant boyfriend or two. All my gals use the group to expand their sensual lives. When you are on staff at the Pussy Palace, you cannot have a mediocre sex life—you have to get it going on. Lori keeps her husband close, but neither would want their marriage to interfere with her flirting. Kadidja gets first dibs on the hot men who come to the courses. And there is a wonderful, ever expanding group of volunteers who float through the Palace every week, including Jackie, Elizabeth, Marianne, Lori G., Elvira, Alina, and Jean, who bring their own special brand of fun and sass.

Women have an incredible ability to turn each other on and inspire each other. Picture going shopping with a girlfriend—you find stuff for her, she finds stuff for you. You encourage each other to try things on. You laugh your heads off and talk each other into things that you might not have tried on your own. When she grabs something sexy, you feel you might try something sexy, too. Your appetites and desires build on each other and grow as you fan each other's flames. Remember that a turned-on woman is in her top form. She is at her best. Her decisions are relevant, her communications are clear and loving, and she is moving in a direction that serves not only herself but her extended family and community. Women get themselves in trouble when they make big life decisions without being turned on or connected to their life-force. The Sister Goddess community is designed to keep a woman continually at her hot and juicy best while she tackles life with both hands.

When they get together, women also give one another freedom and permission to reach for their dreams. There is a certain kind of cutting loose that women do when they are in the presence of other women only, even when a woman is quite at ease among men. When you hear one of your Sister Goddesses talk about how she taught her husband how to kiss every inch of her body, despite her shyness, then her adventurousness opens the doors for every one of the women in her group and encourages them to grab some of that for themselves. Women give women permission to explore their pleasure with as much righteousness as we have been given in the legacy of exploring each other's pain. And that is the invitation here—to use the women in your community to be your companion in your journey to research and explore your potential to create hot, fabulous, intimate partnerships.

Women influence each other whether they like it or not. We influence each other, elevate each other, and help each other believe that whatever we're doing, we're doing it right. I remember one summer, when I was fourteen, my friend Jeannie decided that tree bark was a delicious thing to eat. And so, for that entire summer, my whole gang of girlfriends and I ate bark. We peeled it off trees and put ketchup on it. We thought we were hilarious. We made things out of it. We got other kids to eat it. And we are lucky we did not poison one another. But that is the power of a group of women, and a new concept. Fashion depends on it. When we see our best friend in a pair of Paper jeans, and they look so good on her, then we have to have them. And when our other friends see us in them, they all have to have them, and soon Paper jeans is making millions. There is power in a gang of girlfriends. They can take one woman's pleasure and expand it exponentially. And Mama's goal is for you to take advantage of that power to help you make manifest your greatest desires.

Each of you can put together your own Sister Goddess group of girlfriends who are interested in creating hot, thriving relationship lives and married lives. You may be thinking to yourselves, Mama, I thought it was all about marrying the right *man,* not marrying the right group of *women!* And I hear you, darlings. Just hang with me on this one. It takes a village to train a man. And it takes a village to train a woman to train a man. You think you are going to overcome five thousand years of patriarchal conditioning *by yourself*? Get a grip. Why work that hard? When you surround yourself with women who want the same things you want, and want you to have all the things you desire, you get them much quicker.

We will set up a system of rules that must be followed for participation.

1. Pursue pleasure. It is really key to bond with one another about pleasure rather than problems. We are all uber-equipped in the problem-examination arena. And underequipped to go for pleasure and describe our pleasure. If problem-focusing

was so useful, we would all have problem-free lives by now. This is a time to experiment with going for pleasure! Do something magnificently pleasurable for yourself each day. Make the time!

2. Praise ourselves and our lives. We have a cultural tendency to overlook the good things and concentrate on what is wrong or missing. Your Sister Goddess group exists for the sole purpose of celebrating you and your life. We are each divine and are not permitted any other viewpoint. Your opinion of yourself has huge consequences not only for you but for all the people around you. If you adore yourselves, you will be adored. If you despise yourselves, you will be despised. Since we are actually in control of our lives and our opinions of ourselves, we might as well decide that we are each gorgeous and exquisite and fabulous. We will create better results in our marriages if we feel that way.

3. Appreciate our guys instead of bashing them. Every man lives to serve you and add to your happiness. You may not know this or believe it right now. Your man may not really know exactly what it is that you want—yet. That is okay. The experiment in your life is just beginning. But I will tell you, if you can find something to appreciate about your man, he will want to do even more for you. And if you trash your guy, he will do less and less and have a poor attitude, to boot.

4. Find the perfection in every circumstance. We are all going to experiences challenges. We are all going to have obstacles to

our goals. The trick is to assume that whatever is happening is, in some way, perfect. And to look at it through the lens of finding a way to love whatever is happening and to use it to our advantage.

5. Describe what's working. Most of us were trained to look at things with a critical eye, rather than an appreciative eye. It is much better for your relationship if you keep your eye on what you have, rather than on what's missing.

6. Give up your rights. Your right to be angry, that is. Don't waste your valuable time being furious with him.

7. Don't waste your time trying to solve problems, either. Problem solving rarely leads to solutions—it usually leads to more problems. Look for a way to have fun instead. The problem will solve itself, and you will come to your senses when you pursue your pleasure.

In the next chapter, I will describe these ground rules in more detail. They will help you and the members of your Sisterly Goddess community grow into the most pleasured, sassy, hot, dazzling married women you could possibly imagine. Your group of women can cheer each other on, keep each other in line, run underground missions for one another. Your gang of Sister Goddess girlfriends can assist you in innumerable ways, sometimes even without your asking. Consider this brag from Sister Goddess Pammy, who took advantage of a chance encounter to train the fiancé of her Sister Goddess girlfriend:

I am going to a neighbors' wedding tomorrow. The hubby-to-be stopped me in the park the other day to complain that he was fighting with the wife-to-be because she wanted an automatic transmission on their European rental car for their honeymoon, but it cost $500 extra and they were already close to broke. I flirted with him ever so gently on her behalf, urging him to make his bride happy and give her all she desires. I promised him that it would all return to him twofold if he did so. I am not attracted to this man personally, but it was so much fun to find that I can use my womanly charms in the pursuit of OTHER women's pleasure! This is a great service to the partnered and married women out there! Just think if we all did this for one another.

Just think how the world would be if all women everywhere helped train each other's men! Since it takes a village to train a man, and it takes a village to train a woman to train a man, your Sister Goddess group will provide powerful assistance in your quest to strengthen your marriage.

How to Gather Your Own Sister Goddess Group

To speed you on your way, I want to help you build a network of women, whether it's one other woman or twenty, whether it is your girlfriends, sisters, in-laws, or your coworkers. The idea is to follow these exercises in companionship with one another, so that you can create a support system for your marriage that extends beyond your limitations and reaches what other women of like intentions see as your full-throttle potential for happiness and gratification.

How do you find each other? One group of Sister Goddesses in Atlanta got together by putting an ad in the *Penny Saver* at the local food market. They gather every week to brag. Another group in L.A. all work together. A group in Seattle was in a book club together; they started doing the exercises from *Mama Gena's School of Womanly Arts* and now they read books and have Sister Goddess group meetings. Sister Goddess Lisa from Santa Cruz found her group at her local NIA class, which is a wonderful exercise class that combines movement, martial arts, and music. The women were already in the habit of meeting once a week, so the addition of the Womanly Arts was a natural progression.

You don't have to wait for the right group of women to appear. Just start by yourself. Something interesting will happen to you as you begin this journey toward pleasure. You will attract like-minded women. If you walk into a Starbucks carrying this book, someone might approach you and ask you what you are reading. She would be a good candidate. After a few weeks of doing the exercises, you will become happier. You will begin to have more fun with your husband, and you will notice that your desire will draw in your direction some women whom you did not expect. Someone will comment on your happiness or notice the way you relate to your husband or yourself, and she will ask you about it. She might be a candidate. And you may not even *like* her that much. But she has the same goals that you have, which makes her a valuable ally. You have to leave your prejudice out of the equation as you gather your gang.

You want to include women who are attracted to you and to whom you are attracted, rather than women you have to coerce. Say you have someone in your world who might be a candidate—you aren't sure, but you keep thinking about her. You can tease her a little about what you are doing, telling her you have found something even more fun than the local garden club. Then drop it or withdraw the offer. The most pleasurable way for a woman to operate is to attract, rather than to force. You do not want to coerce someone into participating. You want her to want to.

If you force someone to join you, she will be too much work. She will always rely on you to push her, and then, if she has a problem with her husband, she might blame you for it. Sister Goddess Jessie was one of my first Sister Goddesses. She learned so much from the course and started to enjoy her new life after a divorce so much that her girlfriends noticed the remarkable change in her. One of her pals, Sister Goddess Julie, who was her hairdresser and friend, was going through some boyfriend trouble. Jessie kept telling her things to inspire her, but soon Julie started to rely totally on Jessie for her happiness. When things would nose-dive with her boyfriend, Julie would blame the troubles on Jessie's counsel. This is a situation you want to avoid. It is dangerous to give someone unsolicited advice that she has not made any personal investment in getting. She can start to hate you. That is why it is important for people come to the group of their own free will and with their own goals, to do the homework, and to agree to participate with enthusiasm.

We all have, within us, the ability to reinvent the way we relate to ourselves and to our guys. Redesigning your life around pleasure is a decision, just like going to the gym and exercising is a decision about redesigning your life around a healthy body. What Jessie did, finally, was tell Julie that she was not going to give her any more advice and that it was time that Julie took a class on her own. That worked out to be much better, and now that Julie is up and running on her own, she and Jessie are friends again.

Your Sister Goddess group is going to be about one thing only: celebrating what is good in your life and good in your relationship. You can have other girlfriends to bitch and moan with. I do not want to deprive you. But this gang of gals is here to travel with you on the journey of expanding your pleasure, first and foremost with yourself and, as a consequence of that, in relationship with your husband or boyfriend.

Here is an example of a woman who went for a wonderful celebration of herself which took her, and all of her friends, higher:

I read both of Mama Gena's books during a very low point in my life a few months ago, and thanks to Mama Gena, I have renewed my marriage and resurrected my life. I HAVE FOUND PLEASURE. Wanting to help my sisters feel the same, I threw a "Princess Party" Friday night from 7 to 10 P.M. I decorated with a princess theme—plates, cups, banners—asked all my princesses to wear tiaras and supplied party tiaras to those who didn't wear one. Invitees were also instructed to wear pink or red. I served strawberries and pink champagne (as well as some mean margaritas!), had cheese, chicken tenders, salads, and a Barbie Doll cake. I had hired a belly dancer, who gave a ten-minute demonstration and a twenty-minute lesson. At the conclusion, she said a prayer to reignite the goddess within all of us. All of my CDs were by women artists or about women, i.e., Madonna, "I Will Survive," etc.

As each goddess/princess departed, she received a "princess survival pack" (bags are available with princesses on them). Each contained a sensual pink candle, heart-shaped pink-foil-covered chocolates, tea bags, homemade bathsalts (dyed pink!), and a copy of the goddess mantra from the Mama Gena website (copied in pink and tied with a pink ribbon). Just wanted you to know that it's been three days and everyone is still talking about it. I am launching a monthly potluck gathering out of it. Just wanted to touch base and say thanks for changing my life as I am doing the same for my sister goddesses.

P.S. Several asked me about the inspiration and I gave credit where credit is due and plugged your website and books. Thanks, Mama!

What do you do if you only have cranky, complaining, miserable girlfriends? What if there is not a single woman in your world whom you would feel comfortable even telling that you were on this journey? Well, if you don't feel comfortable talking to a big loser about your desire for happiness, don't. She would just criticize you and try to bring you down. Not good. Some women are simply not at all interested in being anything other than victims. Luckily, the negative types drop out early on. It's kind of like starting a book club: only people who really like to read will join. People who hate reading won't want to be in your book club. You only take the avid readers or the people who want to become avid readers.

If you include women who don't want to have great lives, you may find yourself limiting your joy so as not to offend them. Most of us have a tendency to limit what we are willing to ask for because we feel like we are stuck with the status quo. Or we feel we have to do things his way because he's the man of the household. Or maybe no one else is asking of her husband what we are asking from ours. The limitations that other women set up for themselves will have an effect on us.

After Kara became a Sister Goddess, she felt embarrassed in front of all the other married women at her office. She and her husband of ten years were having so much fun together that he started sending flowers to her office once a week. One day, he even sent over some lingerie from Victoria's Secret. Kara felt awkward about all of this and asked her husband to cool it because the other women at the office did not get that kind of attention from their husbands, and they were accusing her of having an affair. She felt embarrassed that she felt so embarrassed. But Kara hadn't had so much fun with her husband since their engagement. Funny how it's fine to have big displays of adoration when you are just beginning a relationship, but it's considered unnatural by the time you reach your five-year anniversary. Let's see if we can't just turn that around.

Understand that you are not signing up to be everyone's marriage therapist. You aren't even looking to be a Girl Scout troop leader. That's far too much corralling and organizing and hand-holding. The reason for discussing your marriage with your girlfriends is to learn and practice new tools and new language. The tools and the language we have now are insufficient for the task ahead. For example, when we say things like, "He won't let me" or "I can't," we are lying to ourselves in the most insidious way, and this will have destructive consequences on our lives in partnership. No one *needs* anyone. We are each sufficient on our own. We may want a man, we may desire a man, but we do not *need* a man. And no man is responsible if you don't get everything you want. Each of us has the ability to have our way in this wonderful world. If I can help a Sister Goddess redesign the way she speaks about her partner, I can have a Sister Goddess redesign the way she feels about him and relates to him, and consequently, the outcome. A Sister Goddess is not a victim. A Sister Goddess is a woman who knows what she wants and gets what she wants.

Staying the Course (Not Dropping the Group When Things Get Good)

Once your group is up and running, hold on for dear life. One of the great mistakes that women make when a man enters the picture is to give up their group of female friends. They attempt to make him their support system, which is about as effective as breathing carbon monoxide instead of oxygen.

Sister Goddess Jessica, a real Southern belle, came to Mama five years ago, desperate to get married, as she was thirty-five and felt it was time to grab a guy and go for it. She was so attractive and fiery, but she had gotten bogged down in the weight of working hard in the retail clothing industry for the past few years in L.A., and had lost her spark. Connecting with the class each week and bragging began to lift her spirits and remind her exactly who she was and how spectacular she was. On a ski trip to Telluride, she met a fair-haired guy named Allan, from Switzerland, and decided he was the guy for her. She was having so much fun with him that he was hooked instantly, and they were married two years later. As soon as Jessica found Allan, she dropped out of the School of Womanly Arts and dropped her group of Sister Goddess girlfriends. About a year into her marriage, Jessica washed up on Mama's shore, desperate for a fun infusion. She had a great, sexy courtship, a great, sexy wedding, and then she had fallen into the trap that all of us were programmed to fall into—becoming a wife. She stopped doing what she wanted to do, slowed down her social life, spent all her free time and money on hormone shots and calculating the fertile days of her cycle so she could get pregnant immediately, and generally had a very unhappy time. All the fun that had been present before the wedding was gone. Her life was now about fitting into some program of accomplishment that she had in her head, and she judged herself wrong for not fitting.

The first assignment of the week in her marriage course was to write down her vision of marriage, what she grew up thinking it would be, the full-throttle fantasy, complete with theme song. Jessica had been living in unhappiness for so long that, rather than indulge in her fantasy, she used this assignment as a way of writing down all her hurt and anger and sadness and disappointment. It erupted from her like a projectile, and I encouraged her to write it all down and cry her eyes out. A gal has to get all that crap out of her system in order to clear her eyesight and move ahead. She had been holding back the tears and pretending she was happy for so long that the release of this load left her feeling light and free and happy. She felt like herself again, and the naughty little troublemaker that lived inside of her erupted when she went to a party that evening:

A whole gang of my girlfriends and I went out to celebrate my birthday last night. I have not been out with my girlfriends in so long! I really surprised myself with how outrageous I have become since taking this course. All of you Sister Goddesses would have been so proud of me! I gave a copy of Mama's book to ALL of my girlfriends, as party favors. I told them I was taking the class. All of them had heard of Mama, but none of them had ever had the honor of meeting a real, live Sister Goddess! I was wearing a miniskirt with thigh-high stockings and no panties. My husband sat next to me, all night, fingering the top of the thigh highs. None of my girlfriends could believe that this was actually ME. I was willing to be sexy and flirtatious and wild!

When we got home, my husband literally ripped my clothes off! He is not usually the aggressor, sexually, but as soon as he got me in the elevator of our apartment building, he pulled up my skirt and began to slip his fingers into my pussy, slowly circling my clitoris. He pressed stop on the elevator, between floors, and knelt down in front of me and licked my pussy until I was moaning. Then he lifted me up, and we had sex right in the elevator! I have always had a fantasy of being *taken* by my husband in exactly this way.

Jessica was assisted in restoring herself to herself by the exercise and the support and approval of all the Sister Goddesses in her marriage course. She knew that they appreciated and valued her. The Sister Goddesses amplified her confidence and the fun and flirtation in her life. And their presence inspired her, whether she went out alone or with her husband and other friends. Kind of like how being a Girl Scout, when you are a kid, can inspire Girl Scout–like behavior in you even when you are away from your troop. The inspiration that Jessica took from her group was to be true to herself, to have fun, to be as outrageous as she wished, and to celebrate herself—and her husband. This decision elevated Jessica, and it created a lot of fun with her pals at the restaurant.

It is wonderful to have a group of women with whom you can be totally yourself and expose just how outrageous and lusty you actually are. Women adore exposing and celebrating their wild side, in a safe environment, in companionship with one another. When Jessica bragged about her hot sex with her husband, it inspired other Sister Goddesses in her group not only to brag about their sex lives, but to go for more fun with their husbands. We are all a bit competitive. And competition gets a bad name sometimes. But when one uses competition not only to take oneself higher, but also to take one's relationship life higher, that is a wonderful outcome. Jessica's sexy brag inspired all of the women in her group to grab a little extra fun with their husbands that week.

Your Sister Goddess marriage group can also ease your doubts about yourself. Sister Goddess Jessica got married at thirty-seven and had put off having children. She was now forty-one years old. Sister Goddess Mona had also married late, and she and her husband were both very accomplished in their careers. For Mona, her marriage was her priority, not children. When Jessica heard Mona's viewpoint, she felt better about her decision not to have kids, and her doubts about herself evaporated. Doubt is the devil. The devil often gets a front-row seat in a woman's mind and imagination. Doubt can spoil anything it touches, but your Sister Goddess marriage group can create alternatives. When we know we are not alone, doubt evaporates. When we see others making similar choices, doubt vanishes. And we don't realize how our culture encourages us to doubt ourselves as a way of life. When alone, women run a tape of doubt in their heads constantly. We do not even doubt that we should doubt ourselves. So to find confidence where doubt formerly resided is a beautiful, fortifying experience. Pleasure, fun, lust: they are all marvelous replacements!

And when a woman's doubt about herself vanishes, her doubts about her husband also vanish. A guy has a really hard time becoming a hero when the woman in his life is doubting herself or doubting him. Doubting your guy becomes a self-fulfilling prophecy. Believing in your guy also becomes a self-fulfilling prophecy. A few months earlier, Jessica's husband had lost his job as an investment banker. Jessica started to view her husband, Allan, as lazy and unproductive. She began to treat him as if he was a disappointment to her, and insufficient to the task of taking care of her or fulfilling her dreams. As his confidence in himself was eroding, he grew more and more lazy.

So when Jessica started to have more fun, her doubts dissipated, and Allan saw his confidence restored. Suddenly, instead of coming home from work and finding a moping husband still in his pajamas, she found a guy who was eager to take her out to her favorite restaurant for dinner, who was bragging about a fabulous new resume, how he was going to build a house for her, and about the trips they would take together—a man who was feeling excited about life again. So much so, he made plans to go out with the guys for a guys' night out. She was attracted to his newfound confidence, which of course led to even more fun and intimacy.

The Sister Goddess group does nothing more, or less, than hold you accountable to your pleasure. It is a way for a woman to be reminded of exactly how glorious she is and to live in that aspect of herself, which takes her whole world higher. Sister Goddess Jessica originally got her guy because she had tapped into the delicious internal wellspring of being turned on to herself. This is so attractive. We love ourselves when we are all revved up and flush with life. And we are so attractive to others, especially men. And when you choose a guy to be your partner, it is especially important to continue to do whatever it takes to expand your pleasure and fun. Most women cut out at this point and stop stoking their own coals, then blame the guys for the decrease in fun in their lives and in their relationship. Which is what happened to Jessica—she got married and began to live as a married lady, rather than living as a fireball married lady.

Rejoining her Sister Goddess community helped her to jump-start her fun and remember her true self. Neither women nor men have any idea how profoundly important this elixir of life actually is.

As you start assembling your group, remember to be careful of the naysayers. When Sister Goddess Krisztina's marriage was crumbling under the strain of her persistent unhappiness, she became a Sister Goddess by taking a class. She was living in New York at the time. As Krisztina explored her own pleasure—taking candlelit baths, learning about her body, remembering how to flirt, and going out with her girlfriends—she seduced her husband, Steve, into joining her on the discovery of this new world of pleasure. They now have an incredible marriage. They have moved to Connecticut, where she has a beautiful apartment and lives in a Hungarian immigrant community, so she is surrounded by lots of friends. She called me a few weeks ago with the exciting news of her first pregnancy! All would be great, except for one challenge: her group of girlfriends. She comes from a very traditional Eastern European background. In her culture, the woman cooks, cleans, and takes care of the kids. Since becoming a Sister Goddess, Krisztina has found doing all the housework herself is not really that much fun, so she has invited Steve to join her. He now cooks dinner sometimes, cleans the dishes and the kitchen every night, vacuums, and does windows. He enjoys cleaning and especially enjoys making his beautiful wife happy. Her girlfriends are crazy about this, and not in a good way. They are jealous. They think Krisztina has lost her mind and become lazy, and as a consequence, she has created a lot of enemies in her group of friends. They talk about her behind her back and criti-cize her. The icing on the cake was the huge fight she had with them last week at a dinner party when she was talking about how she and Steve were going to share child care once the baby was born. She and Steve had decided to take turns getting up at night with the baby. Her friends went ballistic. "What do you mean, *Steve* will get up with the baby? Aren't you going to do *anything*? You expect him to work while you stay home all day, and then *take care of the baby?* And what will *you* do?"

Krisztina had been my nanny when my daughter, Maggie, was born, and she watched Bruce join me in changing diapers and feed-ing the baby. She rather liked the shared experience of parenting. She had also witnessed the different styles of parenting and part-nership with other Sister Goddesses when she had taken a class. But it was a radical departure for the women of her culture, and having one of their own cut loose and grab a little freedom pissed off her old friends but good. Krisztina is not sure what to do ex-actly. Part of her wants to return to the old ways of her tradition, so she doesn't lose her group of friends. And part of her wants to con-tinue to move ahead in the direction of her pleasure. This is a very tricky spot that all of us have been in, at one time or another, and will be in again as we reorganize our marriages and have more fun with our men.

That is how the international epidemic of low self-esteem among women remains in place. Misery loves its company. It is something that I notice consistently with the women who take my courses.

When they start to boogie at a higher beat, all their old girlfriends attack them for hauling their asses up out of the "I hate myself" muck and into the "I adore myself" sunshine. Kooky, but a factor we must consider. Becoming a Sister Goddess is a courageous business. It's courageous business to lead a pleasurable life. It's courageous business to become friends with a man. But how much fun can life be without a little risk?

So what is Krisztina to do? Give up her old friends and be alone? No, that would not be fun. She can continue to relate with these women for their friendship, companionship, and shared history, but when she wants to relate about issues of man-training, she will have to choose another group of girlfriends. When she wants to be inspired or inspire someone, she can call or visit friends from her days in New York.

A group of Sister Goddesses will serve as an incubator in which you can regenerate your communication style, which will have a huge payoff in your marriage. When you stop practicing being a victim with other women and start to own your life and your destiny, you inevitably interact differently with your man because you are no longer living as though he has the keys to your future. You know you are in the driver's seat.

There are communities of Sister Goddesses all over the world who have graduated from my classes and have formed these groups of on-line and in-person support and expansion. Babies have been born, marriages have taken place, sensual expansion has occurred, and retraining husbands and wives is happening each and every day.

Here are some exercises. You can do them yourself, in a journal, if you do not have a group yet.

1. Have your first phone or in-person meeting. Begin with everyone bragging, telling the group something wonderful about themselves.

2. Have each person bring and read her desire list and talk about the goals that she would like to accomplish with her marriage. (Goals, not complaints.)

3. Have each person describe something she loves about her husband.

4. Describe the hottest moment ever between you and your husband.

5. Brag about a pleasurable thing that you recently did, just for yourself.

6. Set a day and time for your next meeting. Read the next chapter of this book and do the next exercises before the next meeting.

7. Watch the video *Fried Green Tomatoes*. See how Kathy Bates begins to turn her life around and her marriage around with the support, attention, and freedom extended to her through her relationship with Jessica Tandy.

8. Draw a line down the middle of a large piece of paper. Title one side VICTIM and the other side HEROINE. List all the ways you are a victim in your life, and all the ways you are a heroine.

Bring this list to your next Goddess gathering. See if you can find the way in which you are responsible for, and therefore the heroine of, every part of your life in which you are currently victimized.

9. If you do not have a group and want to form one, here are some suggested steps to create your first one.

   - Go everywhere with a copy of this book. Other women who are reading it or interested in reading it may ask you about it. If someone approaches you, ask her if she might like to participate in a group.
   - Put up a sign at your gym, church, synagogue, or the local grocery store.
   - Ask your book club, or moon circle, or the moms from your kids' playgroup if they might like to meet separately to form a Sister Goddess Marriage group with you.
   - Invite your most fun girlfriends to participate.
   - Throw a Goddess Party for your girlfriends.

CHAPTER THREE

The New You in Action

Nobody can be exactly like me. Sometimes I even have trouble doing it.

—Tallulah Bankhead

We all know women who move from marriage to marriage. Each guy inevitably disappoints them. The problem is always *him*. We also know the loud, angry, cranky women who trash their husbands at every opportunity. I am interested in a different kind of marriage—I see, in each of you, the potential to be badass married women who are downright delighted at what they have and what they are capable of creating.

Your happiness is in your hands. There are parts of your marriage that are just ecstatic. Why? Because *your* actions, *your* behavior is consistently positive. If you see all the potential in the world when you look at yourself and at your guy, then you will create that. But then there are aspects of your marriage that are burdensome, unpleasant, and downright hostile. Why? The actions *you* are taking create or allow this burdensome, unpleasant atmosphere. If you see nothing but limitations and restrictions and servitude when you look at your marriage, then, my darlings, you will inevitably create *that.*

This chapter will introduce you to a new way of relating to your husband. By changing your behavior and dedicating yourself to the power of pleasure and positive thought, you can permanently change the dynamic of your relationship. In this chapter we will examine, step by step, how every woman (with a little help from her fellow Sister Goddesses) can change her outlook and change her marriage. Learning new skills to take control of your own behavior does not happen overnight. Assuming responsibility for your relationship happens in baby steps, incrementally, over time.

Mama's Marriage Manual Step #1: Dedicate Yourself to Your Pleasure

The first step is to begin to investigate your pleasure, your desires, and your goals with enthusiasm and the spirit of exploration. When a woman becomes a Sister Goddess and starts to pay attention to her pleasure, it has soul-altering consequences. It is as though her ownership of her ecstatic core elevates and expands her relationship with the divine. The expansion of her inner divinity expands her ability to see the divine and inspire the divine in others. A simple trip to a coffee shop can become a deeply moving, grandiose adventure into the beauty of mankind and the delicious, hot love that is humanity. Life is a resoundingly sensual landscape, filled with heartaching beauty each and every day. When a woman begins to prioritize pleasure, she begins to see it all around her.

Taking care of ourselves and paying attention to our pleasure can be something we forget in times of stress, and in those times your fellow Sister Goddesses will help you help yourself. Sister Goddess Dorothy, for example, is married to a man twenty years older than she is. Her Sister Goddess marriage group pitched in last weekend and helped her sister look after Dorothy's bedridden husband so she could get away for the weekend and pamper herself. Dorothy would never have left her husband's side if it were not for her group.

Dear Sister Goddesses,

Thank you!! I cannot even believe I am the same woman I was a week ago! I feel sexy and delicious and relaxed and somewhat giddy. After the spa, I felt so good when I came home to my husband. Rather than resent him, like usual, I was actually happy to see him. I ran over and gave him a really big smooch, right on the lips. Not a dry peck, like usual. His crankiness vanished. Since I had had such a great weekend of self-pleasuring, my good mood was contagious and my husband caught it! He and I fell asleep laughing and talking, and in each other's arms. Just like the old days.

Thank you all!!

*I*f you want to give pleasure, you have to *know* pleasure. If form indicates function, then each woman is a living roadmap to pleasure, if she follows her design. You were created with eight thousand nerve fibers dedicated to pleasure. In order to live to our capacity as women, we must ignite and maintain our pleasure. When we ignore pleasure, we have miserable lives. When we include pleasure, we have gorgeous, rich, lush, thrilling lives. Pleasure is remembering to put a flower in your hair when you are having a stressful day. It is waking up three minutes early, so you have time to fix your favorite tea in a thermos before your commute. It is laying out your clothes the night before, so when you wake up, it is like you had your very own lady's maid, or taking time each day for sensual self-pleasuring, at home, or at the office. You will resist pleasure, but do it anyway. It is every bit as important as flossing or eating vegetables or paying your bills. In fact, if you ignore pleasure, there is a huge bill to pay at the end of the day.

I had the great privilege and pleasure of spending the summer in a small town on the Jersey Shore. My wonderful town had little musical events at the gazebo in town every night, which I adored. Friday night was disco night, and who did the dancing? Yo Mama, of course, and every kid in town from age two to twenty-two. The grown-up married people all watched from the sidelines. These grown-up married people dance on line-dancing night, and polka night. Why? Well, did you ever see line dancing? The only part of the body that moves, really, are the feet. No hips, no butts, no breasts, no pelvis. That whole area is safely frozen. And polka night is not about hips or butts or breasts, either. It's whirling and stomping. It's as if there is a cultural agreement in America that sexiness, lustiness, and flirtatiousness are for the young and unmarried. And we have even developed dances to keep lust from our midst. You have to be pretty clever and intentional to exterminate sensuality from dancing, but we have done it in America. Call me crazy, but I think the only reason to dance is because it is sexy and sensual and it makes you feel so good to be alive.

I see a direct link between the extermination of lust and the increase of fat. I think if you are not getting yours sensually, you are going to get yours any other way you can. Häagen-Dazs can feel very slippery on the tongue, if you know what I mean. We all know women who start their dating life all sleek and sexy and slim. Then they hook a guy and boom! They get fat and old just as soon as they get married and push out a kid. And it's not just exterior fat. These wives get dumpy and frumpy on the inside. They lack lust. They're lackluster. Lust keeps you young. They possessed that spark right up until the wedding. I want to bring them back to their lusty young selves.

So what are you suggesting here, Mama? A world where old married ladies shake their old married booty? Sounds good. A world where mothers dress in a way that makes them feel beautiful and sensual? Uh-huh. A world where wives and mothers get to flirt and expose their desires and be like Madonna and tongue-kiss their girlfriends Brittany and Christina on the MTV awards? Now we are talking. Why not?

I have a dream that one day the women of this world can sing out loud with their lust, like the birds at dawn. That the desire of women is unleashed and commemorated with the same fervor with which we honor heroes coming home from war. That my daughter will grow into womanhood with the same passion she was born with.

That all the girls and women in the world view their lives as one long celebration of their womanhood and that they treasure every drop of their lust as the elixir of life itself.

And that is the object of your Sister Goddess group. You want to be an excuse for each other to continue to expand each other's pleasure and lust. This may require someone in the group to act as the lust cheerleader. The lust cheerleader may be the first person who has the courage to brag. She may encourage the shy Goddesses to jump in and play the game. The cheerleader role will usually fall to the person in the group who is having the most fun, and that person may change, week in and week out. The goal is to inspire each other to rise higher, rather than for everyone to sink to the lowest common lust denominator. And being the lust cheerleader must never become hard work. It is not therapy or hand-holding. Cheerleading is fun—fun to watch, fun to do. With a rah-rah-rah, a sis boom bah.

This means that there is no room for the determinedly cranky or the determinedly resistant in your group. If a Sister Goddess is too much work, she will probably depart of her own free will. If not, feel free to invite her to leave. You all are together for one reason only—the expansion of fun and lust. You can even use the Sister Goddess pledge that we use at the School of Womanly Arts:

The Sister Goddess Pledge

> *8,000 volts of Pleasure course within me*
> *8,000 volts of Pleasure course within you*
> *Each time I presence my pleasure, I honor us all*
> *Each time I presence my gratitude, I honor us all*

Now why why why is Yo Mama such a devout fan of lust? Because that hot, fun feeling is the juice that gives a human being a reason to be. When two people meet and feel that chemical rush of excitement, the sexual energy is high and everything feels right with the world. Through certain experiences of sensual fulfillment, you feel a sense of unity with eternity, as though you have found your place in the scheme of things and you were born to love and be loved, to feel and be felt. It is an awakening to the pleasure and the gift of being alive. And everyone wants that feeling.

Some people think the feeling can be gotten only with the thrill of meeting someone new or having an illicit affair or sneaking around behind your partner's back. Some argue that a sustained love affair is impossible over time. And only affairs can gratify. The point that this author is missing is that the reason marriage does not stay juicy is that it is not structured to stay that way. It is structured to exterminate juice. If we can let a little desire in the door, we can have an ever refilling vat of juice for a marriage, and lust does not have to come from an affair. A turned-on woman is a woman in her highest state of glory. She is flush with life, vibrant with possibility and enthusiasm. She is aroused with pleasure by her own delicious self, and her world. If we can structure marriage around what turns a woman on, we can create a partnership that continues to sustain its juice, the way an ocean continually creates and sustains waves. You can establish your own juice infusion via the purposeful sharing of sensual information with a group of women whose goal is to lead hot, fabulous lives in companionship with a partner. When Sister Goddesses brag about making pleasure a priority, not only does it add to their pleasure, but it inspires everyone in the group with new ideas of how to go higher with their partners.

Pleasure is, well, a pleasure. It's fun when you have it, it's fun when you think about having it, it's fun when you hear others talk about it. The gift that keeps on giving. For example, last week Sister Goddess Valeria was bragging to her Sister Goddess marriage group about how she had been out to dinner with some friends. She was full from a beautiful meal, and heading home to meet her partner, Cristina. She passed a bakery and saw in the window a piece of cheesecake with strawberries on top. She stopped into the shop and took the cake home to Cristina, who was delighted. She and Cristina put their fingers into the cake and licked the filling off their fingers. They poked the cake again, licking it off, and erupted in gales of laughter as they flirted and licked the cake from their fingers. The Sister Goddesses who were on the phone call all got turned on and giggly with this story. It was a simple story, no acrobatic sex, but it was a delicious event to hear about, to imagine, and to think about. Women are so easy, just hearing something that pleasured or turned on someone else will turn us on. We don't have too many forums for sharing the intimate pleasures of partnership. When you share this kind of information, it serves two purposes—it adds a little thrill to your day when you hear it, and it also fills you with ideas to bring home to your partner. That week, Sister Goddess Erin went out and got a chocolate cake with thick frosting and played a similar game with her husband, Greg. She and her husband had some fun licking the cake off each other's fingers and adding a marvelous little juice infusion to their day and to their intimate relationship.

Taking time out of your highly significant day to talk about cheesecake may seem silly. But I think the divorce rate in this culture is ridiculous. Over half of all marriages end in divorce because no one knows how to keep it fun. And I promise you, you will not divorce a man if you are having live, juicy fun with him. You might divorce someone you are committed to. Commitment means absolutely nothing without fun. And with fun, you have absolutely no need for a commitment: no one leaves anyone if they are having a really good time together.

The object, in a relationship, is to keep the juice alive, not that "first date feeling." That first date feeling is excitement about newness more than anything else. Once you are on your second or your thirtieth date, the newness is gone, but the juice never has to evaporate. The delicious feeling of desire is something that women bring to the relationship, something that we are capable of creating. Your husband cannot supply the juice. You are his supplier. So the group of Sister Goddesses is there to keep you juiced and revved, in your top form to create circumstances that keep you constantly feeling fabulous and enthusiastic about yourself and your life so you have lots of juice to spill over onto him.

Mama wants you, as a woman, to put the same kind of attention and thought to *your* appetites that you put to other people's desires. Explore in detail what nourishes, gratifies, and delights you. We are going to examine all of these topics with exercises in your Sister Goddess study groups.

Marriage Manual Step #2: Praise Yourself

Hallelujah! It is such an almighty pleasure to be a woman. Damn, it makes me crazy it is just so much fun. The privilege of having the body of a woman can just make me collapse in rhapsody all day. I love to look at my reflection in the mirror, seeing my breasts, my legs, my butt, my neck, my pussy. I am forty-seven years old and I think I am gorgeous and I have never looked better in my life. Skin, hair, teeth, lips—it is all so gorgeous. Actually, I have never seen a naked woman I did not love. And I have seen roomfuls of naked women, as those of you who have taken my advanced courses can attest. There is genius in our design. Remember, the same Goddess who designed a sunset designed you. The same Goddess who created the ocean created you. She made an angelfish, and she made your hips. She made the arching neck of a giraffe, ending with those sublime nibbling lips, and she made your languorous arms, stretching above your head as you recline on your pillows. If you can boogie with my rhapsody, you are sane and in your right mind. If you are thinking, *Oh, Mama, that's fine for you but you have never seen my fat ass or my cellulite,* then you are temporarily insane and you must memorize these paragraphs and set them to music.

I want to tell you, sweethearts, you can drive on by and ignore the sunsets that the Goddess has created for your pleasure and enjoyment, or you can pull up a chair and take in the view. I firmly suggest the latter. You have a front-row seat on the most privileged existence: life as a woman. And I want you to suck down every juicy drop. Which starts with the liberal enjoyment of your vessel. Your temple of earthly delights. That hot body you have. It sways, it shimmies, it shakes. I cannot shake it or shimmy it for you. All I can do is invite you to the dance floor. Now get your lazy ass moving.

It's war, sisters. Mama is taking you down. I flat-out cease to permit you to hate your body one moment longer than you have already. Self-loathing sucks the wind right out of your sails. And we require a little wind if we want to make a sea change. Look at loving yourself as a task, rather than something you are supposed to do naturally or something you could do if your body was different. We are reinventing habits that create ecstasy in your hot, sultry little soul. You don't even realize the consequences to your precious soul of the piss-poor habits you currently possess. It is a lazy woman who settles for despising even one small inch of herself. It is a woman who is a genius at the art of living who adores herself wildly, just because she can. Find a way to make the decision, every hour that you are scrumptious. Even if you have to carry a can of Reddi Whip in your glove compartment and lick it off yourself as you sit in traffic. And what on earth do you think a boa is for? It was invented to remind *you* that you are exquisite. Every woman should have at least half a dozen in her wardrobe. Just for work. Bragging is another marvelous way of remembering your gloriousness. You can brag out loud to a friend who appreciates you or to yourself. The recipe works, no matter. Acknowledging wonderful things about other people is also a divine activity. Very uplifting. And when all else fails, a few drops of your secret weapon, Pussy Juice, behind the ears can whisk you instantly to glorious sanity. Worshiping at your own shrine is key and elemental in your marriage, as is your ability to abide in the house of desire, which is your new residence.

Flirtation is another wonderful method of praising yourself and taking on the task of self-adoration as a way of life. Sister Goddess Monica is a successful lawyer who lives in Norwood, Massachusetts, with her sportscaster husband, their two daughters and son. She is a totally fun, outrageous woman with a fabulous sense of humor, but she was not having fun in her marriage. She was in a rut. She was suffering the solitude and boredom of the usual wife/mom/suburbs condition. I don't know about you, but housework, diapers, and nine-to-five just did not get Monica's pussy wet. Not even damp, really. Then an interesting thing happened. During her Sister Goddess class, she began an extensive renovation to her house. Her contractor, Constantine, was around all the time. He was there when Monica got ready for work, when she came home from work, on weekends. He wanted to do whatever Monica wanted to make sure she was happy with his work. Monica rather enjoyed Constantine. Having a man wait on her hand and foot was a wonderful experience. She took to flirting with him, wearing Marabou slippers and lingerie as she pranced around. She found that instead of dreading coming home to the same routine of cooking and cleaning, she looked forward to coming home for a little flirtation with Constantine. An interesting consequence of this experience was that Monica began having more fun in bed with her husband. Hey, she was married, and Constantine was married. Neither of them was interested in disturbing their relationship with their spouse. But the fun, frolicsome, juicy feeling that Monica generated when she flirted with

Constantine spilled over into her marriage and led to some hot encounters with her husband, in the bedroom that Constantine had so recently renovated.

Our culture teaches us that one man, and one man only, is sufficient to gratify a woman. That is the equivalent of saying that bread and water is a healthy diet. Neither man nor woman can live by bread alone. You have to slap a little bacon, lettuce, and tomato between your bread now and then to keep things fun and nutritionally balanced. Are you saying that a married lady should flirt, Mama? With her contractor? You bet I am, sister. With the contractor, the plumber, with all and sundry. Why not embrace whatever turns you on instead of whatever turns you off? Flirtation is in a woman's DNA. We flirt with all manner of things—poodles, babies, girlfriends. If you have a baby and you flirt with someone else's baby, does that make you a bad mother? If you are walking your dog and you kneel down to scratch a neighbor's doggie under the chin, does that make you an unfaithful dog owner? Chill pill. Get a grip. I told you marriage was in need of a makeover. Makeovers are fun, but they also bring with them new requirements and new standards. The standards I am requesting of you do not include immoral or illegal actions; they include allowing the lust that is in your heart to have a little breathing room.

Every woman is a lusty badass. Stuff a lusty badass into an apron in a marriage prison with her husband as jailkeeper, and you are going to have to resort to Prozac or worse to keep her in line. Allow her to breathe and have fun, and you have a partnership for life. So Mama is suggesting you experience all the desire that comes with your package—use your marriage as an excuse to be more of who you are, rather than less.

Marriage Manual Step #3:
Appreciate Your Guy

In addition to the discipline of self-glorification, which I know you are practicing with the same gritty determination that you do your push-ups at the gym, Mama has another little booty-builder for you. It is called appreciation. Most of us have greatly overdeveloped our ability to criticize while leaving our appreciation skills underdeveloped and flabby. We have had years of training in criticism and little to none in appreciation. The one who lives to serve you responds perfectly to both—with appreciation, he becomes even more enthusiastic to give you everything you want, but he gets lethargic and cranky with criticism. And so will you. Criticism gives you wrinkles. Appreciation is a beauty treatment. Your Sister Goddess group serves as your team of personal trainers to remind you to flex your guy-appreciation muscles instead of those wrinkle-causing ones. When I first got together with Bruce, I had no idea how firmly criticism was embedded in my vocabulary and communication style. It took a village to resuscitate me. I owe the joy in my marriage to my village.

Ultimately, you want to use your partnership as a way to explore even more of your beauty and brilliance, rather than your limitations. Criticism limits you; appreciation opens you up to the infinite being that you are. Most women got wired the other way. Sister Goddess Lori had been married to her husband for five years, and they decided to have a baby. She got pregnant when she was forty-two, but it was a difficult pregnancy. She was put on bed rest and ultimately she miscarried. They both were devastated. And they were devastated for many reasons. The loss of the pregnancy was terrible, and they discovered something else about themselves. During the intensity of managing this crisis, Lori and her husband found that their marriage was in terrible shape. They resorted to screaming matches, criticizing and hurting each other. Blame was the name of the game. After her recovery, Lori was up for a major sea change, and she jumped into a coaching program with Mama. She had a custom of constantly criticizing her husband, which was partially due to a communication issue and partially because she viewed her marriage as a way of shrinking, rather than expanding. She yelled at her husband because she was frustrated by the limited life she had created for herself. She was not doing nearly enough of the fun, challenging things that would cause her to grow. She wanted a baby desperately, but she would never be able to clear enough psychic space for one if she did not start having fun with her husband. For her coaching program, we designed all kinds of fun activities and sensual explorations between them. Her husband is a teacher, so Mama would create little report cards for him to fill out. They looked like this:

To heat things up in the fun department for you and your wife, we created a report card for you to fill out and have her bring to her next session. Hope this makes things even more fun for you. Grading scale: A–F.

1. Lori's greeting for you as you come home at the end of your workday. B-
2. Lori's enthusiastic agreement to have a sensual encounter with you, when you suggest it. B-
3. Number of days this week that Lori is fun to be with. B+
4. Lori fulfilling fifteen minutes of naked cuddling time, or together time with her husband, every other day. A-
5. Number of times that Lori insists on having significant talks with you to identify all of your faults, each week. B+
6. Lori seducing you into fun. A

Her husband's comment at the bottom was: *"Great week in spite of personal stress to her. Hot sex!"* He did not like coming to all the sessions, but his feedback and participation was key. Lori began to view her life through the lens of fun, rather than servitude. She and her husband would set up silly dates, like Steak and Blow Job Night (courtesy of the fabulous Sweet Potato Queens), and Lori began to include girls' nights out and weekends away with her friends. A few months later, on September 11, Lori got the news that she was pregnant. They were both crazed with joy. Lori was forty-four years old, and this pregnancy happened naturally, with no interference except increased pleasure and fun in both of their lives. Her husband had always just wanted to make her happy, and now she was over the moon.

Sister Goddess Therese sent out a brag to her Sister Goddess group, describing the consequences of her new appreciation for herself and her husband.

Dear Sister Goddesses,

I had this interesting revelation today about my husband. I have been resenting him for years because I thought he was not interested in me or interested in giving me what I wanted. But I see that the culprit of my unhappiness was me. My husband always has asked me what I wanted, I just never knew what I wanted, so I would get angry at him for asking. I was guilty about having things, guilty about the gifts he offered me, and the gifts he gave me, and guilty about wanting things, and guilty about receiving pleasure from things. I have started to thank my husband for the first time. I look him in the eyes for the first time. I am appreciating him when he walks the dog and takes out the garbage. The first couple of times I tried this, I felt like I was choking on the words, but it has gotten easier as I have practiced. I was used to criticizing him for so many years, I was not accustomed to appreciating him. I never wanted to take responsibility for my pleasure. I wanted him to do it for me. Now I am grateful to be the one responsible for how much fun we have. And it makes me feel good to be gracious and loving with this man that loves me so much. I feel so much better about myself.

Sister Goddess Debbie has a great relationship with her husband, Robert. He desperately wants whatever it is that her heart desires, yet she has been so full of her own negativity that she could not really see that or appreciate him—or herself. One night, while she was taking the Sister Goddess class, Rob wanted to surprise her. He knew she had been busy all day with their three kids, and he knew she had class the next night. He looked at her homework sheet and saw she had to watch a video, *Dangerous Beauty*. Robert went to the video store, got the movie, then went to the small-appliance store where he picked up the microwave oven that Debbie had been wanting for six months but just had not had time to buy for herself. He knew she loved microwave popcorn with her videos. This touched Debbie, but it wasn't until she got to class the next night and bragged about it that she realized exactly how amazing her husband actually is. The other women in class were so impressed with Robert and the attention he showered on Debbie that she recognized exactly how great her marriage actually was, and how Rob is so genuinely supportive of her goals, and how great she must be to have inspired such devotion. Debbie had a great thing going on with Rob, but she was not enjoying it to the fullest because she was being ruled by the regulation doubt that is our cultural inheritance. Rather than approving of herself or appreciating Rob, she was constantly wondering, Am I a good wife and mother? Did I send the right gift to my sister-in-law? Did I make the right impression at the business dinner we hosted last night? Did I choose the right school for my daughter? The people who pay the highest price for our doubt, besides us, are our husbands.

This realization gave Debbie new confidence in herself. She began to make it a daily practice to appreciate herself and her husband. The family lived in a tiny two-bedroom apartment in New York City, with three children under the age of six. They had long since outgrown their home, which was wall-to-wall toys and stuff. With this newfound trust in herself and her relationship, Debbie made a bold move. When she was visiting her friend in Westchester, she took it into her head to go house-hunting, since the house next door to her friend was for sale. She fell head over heels in love with the huge amount of space and the backyard. She had been an enthusiastic New Yorker for so long that she could barely believe herself, but she and Robert put in a bid on the big house and got it. Her tiny New York City apartment sold for exactly the same price as this big house, and within a few months, Debbie had moved the family to a beautiful new home. A man and a woman can get so good at following a woman's desires that they can create miracles together.

Mama's Marriage Manual Step #4: Find the Perfection in Every Circumstance

Most of us grew up thinking that the world is divided into good and bad, right and wrong. In the world of the Goddess, life is different. There is no right or wrong. In fact, everything that happens has perfection to it. When we look for what is wrong or missing, we often overlook what we have. We keep comparing our husbands to old boyfriends or the guy in our imagination or the guy our sister has or the guy our parents wanted for us. Until he gives us the jewelry we want or the house we deserve, or until he gets the right job, we withhold our approval. We don't even see the guy we are with. And there is no way to get to happiness or appreciation from there.

What do you do when you look around you, and nothing seems good or sufficient? You change your frame of reference by looking for the perfection, instead of the problem. Sister Goddess Grace was with her boyfriend, Ricardo, for five years. During that time, she kept pressing him to resolve his divorce, so he could marry her, and they could have a baby. Ricardo said he would marry her in a minute, if not for his children. He was separated from his wife, but how could he possibly leave his children? He always treated Grace as if she was second best in his world. And because Grace thought she was, she felt comfortable in that role. She kept waiting patiently for Ricardo to make his plans to be with her, she kept doing things to please him, and yet she was getting impatient. Grace was never comfortable in the role of being second best. She knew it was wrong but she was stuck. She just didn't have the self-worth and love of herself to believe she could do better.

When Grace first came to me, she wanted to convince Ricardo to marry her. She thought he was the one. I suggested to Grace that if that was indeed her goal, rather than finding Ricardo wrong all the time, she could find his indecision right. Maybe he was actually serving her by not marrying her. Grace could not compute. She could not see the perfection of his withholding the ring and the baby she wanted so much. She wanted to stuff Ricardo into her vision, rather than surrender to the perfection of what was happening. I told her we would try an experiment of looking for the perfection for only one week. Ricardo was going out of town to see his almost ex-wife and children. Grace told him she would like to date while he was gone. She explained that while he was still only separated from his wife, she would continue to date around, and her hope would be that one day they would be able to be together. Ricardo agreed, and Grace started shopping. She was shopping from her new vantage point: instead of just being Ricardo's number-two girlfriend, she began to treat herself like a Goddess. She invested in her pleasure. She took care of herself. She took stock of what she had—a great business, great beauty, talent, and passion. The Mama 101 course changed her life. She wrote a love poem, to herself, which she read aloud to all of her Sister Goddeses at graduation.

A Woman's Birthright—A Love Note to Myself

My darling Precious beauty
You are a Botticelli painting
Or perhaps a dignified Monet.
Your wit and intelligence astound me,
Your grace paves the way—for a life filled with ecstasy.
My body trembles at your touch.
I love you oh so very much.
Your passion and your sensual ways have left an indelible mark on my
    soul
And I will cherish you for all of my days.
I long to be with you, I long to stay . . .
I long to sing to you and recite poetry to you each and every day.
Let me pamper you and fill your world with the most beautiful flowers
Morning noon and night—wouldn't that be the most delightful sight!

You, gorgeous goddess, sensual woman, don't you know it's true.
You beautiful, sensitive generous soul whose time is now,
Whose time is ripe.
You luscious pear-shaped woman—know the magnitude of thy being.
Never fill thy heart with doubt, spew it out—just SPEW-IT-OUT.
You vivacious charismatic woman, don't let ANYONE bring you down.
Don't let them even make a sound.
For there is no room in your life for strife.
You, glorious being, sparkling child of God,
Claim your birthright, claim desire.
Let that feeling take you higher
And don't you ever, ever, ever, look back.

With much love and gratitude,
Sister Goddess Grace XOX

The first night she went out, she met a guy who fell head over heels for her. She liked him, but it was more fun than anything. He bought her a ring she had always wanted from Tiffany's. This was such a good experience for her to feel adored and treated like a priority by a guy. The next week she was out again and met a man named Anton. He was seven years younger than she was, and an architect from London. She really liked him. He treated her like a queen, which she was not at all accustomed to. It made her think something was wrong with Anton because Ricardo had never been so good to her. But we were still playing the perfection game.

Mama told her to find the perfection in the way Ricardo treated her and in the way Anton treated her. In fact, if Ricardo had not treated her the way he did, she would never have met Anton. She began to notice that she liked being called every day. She liked having a man spoil her. While she still was turned on sexually by her bad boy, Ricardo, she was also turned on by Anton treating her like a priority. There is a certain kind of chemistry that a woman feels for a man when she knows she is doing something illicit or dangerous. There was an exciting thrill to her encounters with Ricardo because each time they got together, she was sleeping with an officially married man, and she was also trying to change his mind and prove to him that she was even more fun than he'd ever had with his almost-ex. There is a thrill to "let me prove it to you" sex. The thrill of excitement. Grace was not accustomed to "let me worship you" sex, which is what she had with Anton. But we are still playing with perfection here. So I suggested to Grace that she continue with both, just to see.

She began to notice how poorly Ricardo was actually treating her. He would not even open the door to a restaurant for her, telling her she was perfectly capable of doing it herself. It was Anton's pleasure to open doors, order for her, send her flowers, pick her up, drop her off—whatever he could do to add to her happiness. He wanted to marry her and give her a child. He had never been so certain of anything in his life. During this time, Grace went off the pill, in hopes that she would prepare her body for pregnancy. She was forty years old and her periods did not return right away. She was diagnosed with early menopause, which scared her. But we were playing the perfection game. So Mama suggested that yes, it was possible that she would never have a child, but then again, it was possible the doctors were wrong, and she should just keep going for it, and maybe without that diagnosis, she would not have been as motivated to pursue her dreams.

Grace planned a trip to London, where she met Anton's family. He came to New York to meet hers and asked her father for her hand in marriage. While she was there, she saw Ricardo, who was his usual self-absorbed self. Grace was beginning to see how great it was that this man, whom she had been clutching on to for five years, had resisted her every step of the way. It was like he had done her a favor by not divorcing, and marrying her. She would never have had the experience of being adored and treated as a priority by Anton if she had stayed with him. Grace went on vacation with Anton a few weeks later, and, against all odds, became pregnant. They are both over the moon with happiness. They got married last month.

If Grace had still been engaged in the game of trying to fix Ricardo, or prove something to him, she would never have opened herself to the possibilities that led to Anton. There is freedom in perfection, movement, motion. There is stagnation in finding yourself wrong, or finding your circumstances wrong, or trying to force any issue. Perfection is using your innate ability to approve, to your own advantage. You get to live in your own radiance, and see what blooms.

Mama's Marriage Manual Step #5: Describe What's Working

Our attention is a powerful tool. If we put our attention on what is wonderful in our lives, the wonderful part of our lives will expand. If we put our attention on what is missing, we will begin to see and experience what we don't have, rather than what we have. Our language is a tool that we can each use for our own benefit or our own detriment.

One couple began to see me after experiencing a huge change in their lives and in their marriage. About three years ago, Peter, an investment banker, decided to take a really big risk. He invested all their money in ImClone, as he was certain they could make a killing in the market and not only live the life of their dreams, but even beyond their dreams. Peter had spent his entire forty-five years studying the market, and he was as certain of this decision as he had ever been. Within days, the market crashed and the stock market boom was over. They lost everything. Lenore and Peter went from being one of the wealthiest families in Beverly Hills to being millions of dollars in debt to the IRS. For the last three years, they have been living a horrifying charade. Each month they sink further into debt as their expenses outweigh their income. They are in danger of having their house repossessed. They have borrowed from anyone who would lend them money, and their friends and family are no longer willing to bail them out. The worst consequence of all is the growing chasm of hostility that exists between the two of them. To say that

Lenore is furious would be an understatement. She is humiliated every day as she drives her three kids to Beverly Hills High in a ten-year-old Honda, instead of her repossessed Mercedes. She can't stand that she can no longer shop or vacation. And she is so angry with Peter for putting her in this position.

Peter is basically the walking wounded. He is swirling in disappointment and can barely stand being in his own skin. On top of his own shock at his own failure, he has the additional burden of his wife's unhappiness and blame, which have made him numb and isolated, like a wounded dog.

When I first met with these two coconuts, they were each bursting with intense hostility toward one another. They said they wanted to resuscitate their marriage, but they had a bad habit of continually attacking each other verbally. Since nothing good can grow in such a hostile climate, I gave them an assignment of creating an island of time together in which they did something fun, instead of fulfilling any obligation. They were to take a baby step toward rebuilding their friendship, as a marriage is of no value without a foundation of friendship. When they came back to see me a week later, I asked for a report. Each of them was so habituated to the communication style of examining what was missing and blaming each other that they barely discussed the fact that they had gotten all dressed up, gone out to dinner together, come back home, and made love. They wanted to report to me what was still wrong or missing, or what the other had done that was hurtful or insufficient. Our communication styles are habituated behaviors that require renovation in order to design new outcomes. Despite the turmoil in their lives, I insisted that each of them articulate for at least one moment what had been pleasurable in their evening together.

Lenore reported that Peter had taken her to dinner but that she had had to make the reservation herself. I stopped her and asked her to restate that, leaving out the disappointment. She did, simply reporting that Peter had taken her to dinner. She added that he lit some candles when they came home. Then she tried to slip in some comments about his insufficient lovemaking skills. I stopped her and had her re-create the sentence, describing only the good moments. It turned out that she and Peter sat on the bed together, just talking and cuddling for a while. When she reached up to touch his face, he pulled her in for a passionate kiss, and they made love. This event was a perfectly wonderful step in the direction of the closeness and intimacy they both wanted, if they did not diminish it by pointing out what was missing.

This technique is important, not just for your communications with your partner, but in your Sister Goddess groups as well. You have to be willing to be rather precise with one another about keeping the crap out of your communications. One bad apple ruins the bushel, and you have worked much too hard at harvesting your bushel to invite in some silly rotten apple. Describing what is working is pressing the gas pedal of fun and intimacy with your partner. Describing what is wrong or missing is like slamming on the brakes. Not only is it dangerous to slam on the brakes, but it inhibits your progress. So cut it out and spend your time harvesting the ripe, sweet fruit of what is working between you, and share that with your Sister Goddess group. You are going to get better and better at seeing how you track the dirt into your communications. You will also begin to see how your Sister Goddess girlfriends do the same, and you can gently point it out to one another by having them restate their comments.

Mama's Marriage Manual Step #6: Give Up Your Rights

But Mama, what are we to do when our husband *has* been an idiot? When he *has* committed an *unpardonable* act? When we are just so furious we could spit nails right at the bulge below his belt? I mean, didn't Lenore have a *right* to be furious with Peter?

Come on, darlings, you know what you do. You yell at him like you were a screaming fury from the bowels of hell. Or you seethe for days, steam wafting out of you like a viper from Hades while pretending to be Glenda, the Good Witch from the North. Or you sob uncontrollably like a frightened, hysterical child who lost her mommy at Macy's during Christmas rush.

You can try all those tactics if you wish, if they work for you. Personally, after trying all of the above, and then some, I have come to the conclusion that they promote wrinkles in the wrong places, and therefore I no longer indulge.

Try giving up your rights instead. See, most of us grew up thinking that if someone pisses us off or disappoints us, we have a *right* to yell at them or a *right* to be angry with them. And there is no such thing as a *right*. A right is a wound waiting to happen. Hey, we don't even have the *right* to live. Life is a gift. And if life is a gift, it is up to you to decide how you want to spend that gift. Do you want to pour your energy into hate and revenge? Or do you want to pour your energy into expanding your pleasure?

For those of you who want to get to pleasure quicker, an exercise called Spring Cleaning has the ability to rid you of the negative feelings you are experiencing in order for you to be able to communicate what it is that you want from your partner. For example, Lenore and Peter had been communicating nothing but their anger, fear, and disappointment with one another for three years. They actually want to rebuild their friendship and their marriage, but they do not know how to handle all of the negativity that they feel, so they keep tossing it back and forth, not realizing it is tearing away at their foundations. If there were a way to dump the intense negativity, all that would be left would be the love and the open communication about what it is they each want. Telling each other the truth, without the negative charge, is the best way for a relationship to develop.

The best way to do the Spring Cleaning exercise is to pair up with someone in your Sister Goddess group. The idea is to use a member of the group as your partner for this exercise, rather than your husband. Mama wants you to have a safe place to dump your negative feelings for your spouse so that you can communicate your truth nicely. You can do this exercise in person or on the phone. You may want to do this exercise daily if you are going through a stressful time. Your mind has a limited capacity to store negativity. After a certain amount, it just seeps out and takes over everything in the same way a drop of cyanide can poison a whole barrel of water. The idea of this exercise is to rid your mind of the cluttering and oppressive feelings of negativity, so you can head back on the trail of your pleasure and your desires. Anger is not a permanent condition unless you let it take you over.

You will want to do this exercise frequently in order to clean your mental closet of all the dust balls, lint, and collected crap from the months and years of undelivered thoughts and communications. When you don't clean your closet (or your mind) of all the old accumulated junk, you cannot enjoy the nice things you have or make room for new goodies. This exercise clears your mind of all the old yucky stuff so you can be open and receptive to new desires. You can do this exercise by yourself or with a partner from your group or with the whole group.

Spring Cleaning Alone

A Sister Goddess sits by herself and does this process aloud. She questions herself in a simple, expressionless manner and then answers herself. For example:

> S.G. *asks: What do you have on your husband* [use actual name]?
>
> S.G. answers: I am angry that you left your dishes in the sink this morning before work.
>
> S.G. *asks: What do you have on your husband?*
>
> S.G. answers: I loved the way you held my hand at the baseball game last night.

S.G. asks: What do you have on your husband?

S.G. answers: I am in deep despair over the fact we have not had sex in three months.

Spring Cleaning with a Partner

You both must agree to keep confidential everything that you say in this exercise. It is imperative to have a safe environment to look inside yourself. You must not even discuss the content of what was revealed in the exercise with each other at the end of the session. We just want to make a safe space for you to dump all of your old thoughts and feelings. Find a private place and sit facing each other. One Sister Goddess asks the other the same question, over and over, for ten or fifteen minutes, using a calm, unemotional voice. The other Sister Goddess answers. Then they switch. For example:

S. G. 1: What do you have on your husband [use actual name]?

S.G. 2: I am so upset that he forgot my birthday yesterday.

S.G. 1: Thank you. What do you have on your husband?

S.G. 2: He did not even get me a card.

S.G. 1: Thank you. What do you have on your husband?

S.G. 2: I was thinking about reminding him on Monday, but I just wanted to see what would happen.

S.G. 1: Thank you.

Spring Cleaning with Your Group

When three or more women participate in this exercise, one of the women agrees to be the monitor. She goes around the room asking each Goddess, "What do you have on your husband?" In this case, just use the word *husband,* not his name. At the conclusion of this exercise, another Sister Goddess might return the favor and monitor for her. Do the exercise for at least twenty minutes. You will feel free and fabulously energized when everyone has cleaned her mental closet. You can do this exercise with your group each week on the topic of your husbands.

Sister Goddess Lenore began a daily program of Spring Cleaning. One of the reasons that she had been so exhausted, angry, and devoid of humor was that she had let herself be eaten away by negativity for three years. She found an immediate sense of relief after just a few days of Spring Cleaning. She began to feel like herself again. Her natural enthusiasm and joy had just been buried under layers of anger.

Mama's Marriage Manual Step #7: Don't Try to Solve Problems—Go for the Fun Instead

Oddly, this is one of the most challenging requests I am going to make of you. It is simple in its description, and complicated in its execution. It is as if I was giving you a tennis lesson, and I asked you to change your grip on the racket. You could probably understand my point intellectually, but it would feel awkward at first to use this new grip, as it just wouldn't feel like *your* grip. We have so much training in our approach to problem solving and it is so widely accepted that we don't even consider other choices. When a problem comes up in our lives, or our marriages, we immediately look for someone to blame. Then we either internalize the hostility we feel or express the hostility to the person we believe has wronged us. Very often we feel we have the right to dump all of our negative feelings on this targeted individual because of his mistake or our perception of his mistake. The blame game is currently as popular as apple pie and used with abandon by couples throughout the nation—businesses and corporations and international leaders resort to it as well. Everyone you know will back you up if you are an enthusiastic player in blaming your man for his real or imagined affronts.

Except Yo Mama. I think blame is so *last year.* Focusing on what's wrong or what's missing is just so *last week.* Dwelling in the problem and examining the problem is so *yesterday.* I want to offer you something fresh and new and fabulous. Don't try to solve all your problems from the swirling vortex of the problem. Go for some fun. Right now. No questions asked. You are pissed at him? Great—go have yourself some pleasure. He totally messed up? Cool—grab him and go for a little fun with one another.

Hast thou lost thy mind, *chère maman?*

Hear me out, tootsies. When your panties are firmly in a knot over some offense or other, you are temporarily insane. A bull that is raging makes very different decisions than a bull that is calmly grazing in the pasture. I want you to have the benefit of your own sweet genius as you approach important decisions and crossroads in your life, rather than being plugged into your own hysteria. By the way, once you can loft yourself up into pleasure, you will have the most fantastic ideas and insights about whatever you thought your problems were. You will be able to use every crossroad to go for more pleasure with yourself and your partner.

What does Mama mean by this? Our culture is hooked on problem solving. When something goes wrong, our tendency is to pounce on the problem and chew on it, like a dog and his favorite bone. We wrestle, we bite, we tear. And what do we end up with? More problems. We are trained to be the Problem Police on Problem Patrol. Sister Goddess Cindy, from Ohio, was going through a stressful time. She had three kids, ages seven, three, and six months, and a part-time job as an accountant. She was renovating her new house in the Akron environs and was developing her own business on the side. As soon as she came home from work, she was nursing her baby and cooking dinner, usually by herself because her husband worked late. One day she found herself in the kitchen, making dinner and feeling weirdly paranoid, as though her hands were not part of her body. She got scared and ran to her doctor. He prescribed an antidepressant and therapy. The therapist asked her all kinds of questions about the problems in her past, her marriage, and her job. She began to get angry at her mother, her father, her boss, her job situation, her kids, and especially her husband. She was no happier than when she started, and she was aware, more than ever, of her problems. She had to look for the root of the problem and figure out why she had the problem, where the problem came from, and when the problem first started. I am not saying this is wrong. I am just saying this does not lead to fun. At least, not the kind of hot, juicy fun that interests Mama.

After six weeks of this, she came to the School of Womanly Arts. Mama put her in a class. Since she had been so isolated from other women because of her schedule and lifestyle, she needed a juice infusion. Mama had her self-pleasure every day, or have a sensual time with her husband to handle her tumescence. Within a week, this bundle of energy was flying high with her full plate, rather than teetering on the edge of sanity. Fun is simply more fun than problem solving. Fun is energy-giving and life-expanding.

Let's see how all these rules come together. Phoebe and Evan had just about beaten the pulp right out of themselves and each other when they crossed the threshold of the Pussy Palace. As we began our coaching, I explained to them that this was not going to be a long-drawn-out investigation into why Evan had made poor financial decisions or how cruel Phoebe had been to him. This was going to be a quest to find the exquisite adventure and unfolding love-story potential in this leg of their journey together as husband and wife. They had been college sweethearts, having met freshman year. They were in their twenty-fifth year of marriage, and the only outcome I was interested in was leading them each to more fun, either together, which would be my preference, or apart. I told them that this discipline might not be for them, as I was not going to play the blame game. If we were to work together it would be all about how to find the fun and pleasure and perfection, from *here.* And not everyone is interested in that. But since they had come to me after two long years of blaming each other, with no end in sight, they were up for a new direction.

The first step of our work was to *find the perfection* in what was happening. They began to see the loss of income as an opportunity to be creative with their decisions, their work lives, their family, and their time together. Phoebe wanted to finally use her teaching degree, as her kids were all in high school and college. Evan had an idea about a business he had always wanted to start. They realized how many of their friends and family were not really friends but hangers-on to their coattails, and they were glad to be free of them. In *describing what was working,* they saw how relieved they were to be out of the high-pressure, artificial social scene that had taken up so much of their precious free time. One night they declined to attend their night at the opera simply to hang out together in their hot tub, look at the stars, and talk. Evan started to realize how much they loved spending time with one another, and they were determined to design lives that allowed them to be together more. Each of them maintained weekly Spring Cleaning exercises to dump all the negativity that had been taking up space in their minds, and now they were flexing their new ability to *avoid problems and go for the fun instead.* This was most challenging—and most rewarding.

Evan decided that they should use the excuse of their shrinking finances to expand their sex lives. He got quite adept at seducing Phoebe, especially when she was exasperated. He would say, "Mama says whenever you're cranky, it means you want some." And he would throw her down on the bed or the kitchen counter and practice his Extended Massive Orgasm techniques, or just nibble her somewhere. Phoebe decided to make pleasure her new hobby, and every day she would plan fun little activities for herself. Monday she slipped love notes into everyone's pockets. Tuesday she made pancakes for the family in the shape of tushies and boobies. Wednesday she had to work on their tax return, so she wore an evening gown and rhinestone sandals all day. Her life became more about *her,* rather than trying to please or accommodate others.

Evan and Phoebe were just discovering the real potential of their love affair. A lifetime friendship with a partner by your side, looking in the direction of pleasure with you, is an exquisite adventure. It requires a tremendous amount of discipline to be the source of such a love affair, but the rewards are beyond measure. And to have a group of Sister Goddesses by your side as you unfold your love affair is all the lubrication you require to catapult yourself to your dreams with your man.

Exercise #1: The Lust Monitor

This week your job is to be the lust monitor. Your goal is to remain as turned on as possible, as often as possible. Lust is the new morality. Bow before the flames of your desires. For example, Sister Goddess Debbie and her husband, Rob, went to a business conference last weekend. It was their first overnight getaway in years. When they got to the hotel, the desk clerk offered them a room with two twin beds. He said that was all that was available. Debbie said, "What? My first night away from my three kids in two years? Isn't there anything you could do for us?" The beleaguered clerk searched his computer screen in vain, offering them a king-sized bed in a smoking room, which Debbie found unacceptable. She never lost her temper, nor did she give up. She asked him if someone else could be switched or if there was another hotel in the area that could accommodate them. "I really don't think you want us to spend our one night in twin beds, do you?" she asked. "Why don't we go to the bar and have a drink while you see what you can do?" The clerk came to find them twenty minutes later with a key to the bridal suite on the top floor of the hotel. The bellhop took them up to their room, and what did they find? A bottle of champagne, four chocolate-dipped strawberries, and a note from the clerk telling them he hoped they would have a good time!

Exercise #2: Finding Joy

Choose one of the activities that you used to engage in that brings you joy. Add the activity to your week. You may not feel like it, you may not want to, your inner voice may be screaming, "No, no, no. I can't go party with my girlfriends. I am with a partner now!" "I don't have time." "I need to be there for the kids." Do it anyway. Notice how you feel toward your partner after you attend the activity. For example, Sister Goddess Emily from Birmingham, Alabama, had given up her career as a police officer when she had her kids four years ago. She wanted to go back to school to study the latest computer techniques in her field, but she had the idea that her husband would be totally unable to function without her. She did not think he would be happy if she went to school two nights a week, even though they had a babysitter to help him get the kids ready for bed. After thinking long and hard, Emily finally went for it. The fun and enthusiasm that infused her when she was surrounded by new people, new ideas, and new challenges added a great boost to her marriage. Jordon enjoyed seeing this joyful side of his wife emerge, which more than made up for the inconvenience. Emily's bold step left them both happier.

Exercise #3: Describe Yourself

Write a paragraph describing yourself. Use the same proud perspective that a new mom uses when she describes the little niblet toes of her newborn, as if they were the first set of niblet toes on earth. Use only a positive viewpoint to describe all of your characteristics. Are you someone who is serious? Full of joy? What are your talents? Your challenges? Write it up, remembering it is all wonderful.

Exercise #4: Brag

Do one pleasurable thing for yourself each day and brag about it to your group. This will inspire your whole group to expand the pleasurable attention they give to themselves.

Exercise #5: Homework

Turn on the group by describing a hot moment you had with your husband.

Exercise #6: Video of the Week

Watch *The Banger Sisters* with Goldie Hawn and Susan Sarandon. See how Susan has shrunk herself to be in her marriage and how she begins to expand once her girlfriend comes back into her life.

CHAPTER FOUR

❧

Husband Training

A hard man is good to find.
—Mae West

Can your husband be your best, most intimate girlfriend? Can he constantly inspire you with new ideas? Can he intuitively know what you like and don't like? No? Well, what exactly is he for anyway? The previous chapter gave some pointers about controlling your own behavior. Now we'll talk a little about controlling his. Mama will explain the basic principles of owning and operating your man when you're in a committed relationship. I want you to train your man, not change your man. I want to capitalize on his talents and his strengths and maneuver him into the most useful and pleasurable position for both of you. I want you to have a best friend that you have sex with. I want your partner to be the person who knows you the best.

Training is always, essentially, about retraining. After all, he has come to you with a certain amount of training already in place (just as you have come to him with your ability to train already in place).

His mom had a hand in his training, as did all of his previous girl-friends and his sisters. Likewise, your mom and all the women in your world had a hand in your training, simply by allowing you to observe how much marriage either limited or expanded their lives. I am suggesting that you take a road much less traveled. You have the potential to pioneer a relationship in which the pleasure is limitless and continually unfolding. If you are vigilant, you will become the role models for the next generations.

The object of retraining, or husband training, is to view wher-ever you are as an opportunity, rather than a fixed ending with no fu-ture, no possibility. Husband training requires cockeyed optimism. It requires a killer sense of humor. It requires courage. It requires an ability to find the fun, perfection, joy, possibility, potential, and laughter in every situation. If you are not interested in this perspec-tive, you will never become a killer man-trainer. If you know you will always get your way, then guess what? You will always get your way, or better than your way.

It is easy to have optimism, humor, courage, and fun on a first date, a second date, or even for a few weeks or months. There are all kinds of reasons to hope! This guy may be the one! You look at him and think, Oh my goddess, so much potential! I can do so much with this guy! He will be putty in my hands! Then over time, year in, year out, decade in, decade out, the putty turns to bedrock, and you feel as if a stick of dynamite wouldn't move this man. While you were dating, the quirky way he sleeps with his cell phone seemed adorable and so responsible. Now that you're married, you hate that fucking phone and the man who is sleeping with it. He feels your animosity and clings firmly to his cell.

Married couples get fixed into ruts with really deep grooves. You can predict with certainty how he will walk in from work, ignore you and the kids, and pick up the channel changer. Or if he leaves that toilet seat up one more time, you will choke him (but you never tell him so). Or you go out to dinner and he orders for himself first, ignoring you, then shovels his food once it arrives at the table. All of these characteristics can be either grounds for assassination or opportunities for training. You can either look at him and think, *My husband is impossible!* or you can see his potential. The advantage of your Sister Goddess marriage group is that one of your Sister Goddesses might be able to see your husband's potential in areas in which you have abandoned hope. We can't always see the ruts we are in, but when someone gives us a new perspective, we have a shot at hauling ourselves up to enjoy the vista.

Sister Goddess Ebony left the celebration of her first anniversary up to her husband, Sean. She had this idea that he would take her to some romantic restaurant and give her some romantic gift; afterwards they would return home to a candlelit bedroom, where they would make passionate, romantic love. Sean had never had to plan an anniversary before. He had no idea what Ebony wanted.

He was a little nervous, but up to the challenge. He had no clue how important this milestone was to Ebony. No one had informed him that it was also a pass/fail exam in her eyes. Ebony was viewing this as a demonstration of how much Sean loved her. Like a lamb to the slaughter, Sean took Ebony out to the local neighborhood place they go to every week. He wanted to buy her a present but was afraid to shop without her, so he told her of his intentions while she sat opposite him, stewing in her anger over the same pasta special she always orders, at this place they *always* go.

When they returned home, Ebony was way too pissed off to want to make love, so she called her Sister Goddess girlfriend Jennifer, instead. Ebony was practically sobbing at the insufficiency of the celebration. "He doesn't love me anymore!" she wept. Jennifer said, "Oh, Ebony. You have no idea how good you have it. On our first anniversary, my husband didn't even *remember* the date. Sean not only remembered, but he took you out! He wants to buy you something wonderful! It is a great start!" Jennifer was able to talk Ebony off the ledge, and together they cooked up this little scheme to give Sean a second chance. Ebony told Sean everything she really wanted, and the next week, he did the whole anniversary all over again, this time surpassing her expectations. They ended up having the best time and the hottest sensual encounter of their lives. A little emergency help from your Sister Goddess girlfriends can keep your pleasure right on track.

Your fellow Sister Goddesses will be there to help you become that big, badass expert husband trainer. Take, for example, Sister Goddess Donna. She married Daniel, a famous actor, who was twenty years older than she was. She just assumed he would become less and less able to physically gratify her over time. She believed that his sex drive was declining and she would just have to begin to settle for less sex than she wanted, as he was sixty and she was thirty-nine. The fun she had with her Sister Goddess marriage group got her so revved up and juicy that she was able to pull her old guy out of retirement and have the hottest sex of their lives.

Sister Goddess Mary was dealing with her husband's colon cancer. She had forgotten herself in the very real challenges of managing the disease. Her Sister Goddesses took her out partying and she ended up being the only fifty-year-old woman to dance on the bar that night. The jukebox was playing early Tina Turner. You can't stay in your seat for "Proud Mary." Mary would have never even thought of going out were it not for her Sister Goddess marriage group. It took a gang of girlfriends to remind Mary to party and to force her out the door.

Is It Possible to Teach Old Dogs New Tricks?

Is every single husband trainable? Or is it possible that you have got yourself one big bad mongrel that just needs to be put down? How can you tell when it is time to send him back to the pound? It depends on you and your pleasure. If you are still having fun with this man, keep him and train him. If you find yourself complaining all the time and not caring to notice anything positive about him except that you treasure the time you spend apart from him, put him down. Let some other woman have him. There is no prize given for emotional stamina or suffering in a marriage.

Your job, should you choose to accept it, is to take him wherever he is and drive him down the highway of your desires. You can do this. I know you can. You suspect there's absolutely no way out of this marriage prison, but do not lose heart. That no-way-out feeling is only a temporary condition. You have Mama in your corner now. I believe in you. You are a born man-trainer. We are just going to get a bit more deliberate about pursuing happiness. The idea is to look at your current situation as a leaping-off point and to be willing to go bit by bit, with baby steps, in the direction of your goals.

My worst man-trainers are the whining, victimized women who get distracted by their own anger or disappointment and give up on their goals, then blame their guy for it. These women stew in the juices of revenge, rather than wallowing in the fulfillment of their desires. Trouble is, we have so many women stewing in the juices and so few wallowing that majority rules at this time. Sister Goddess Carrie, from Tulsa, has been married for seven years. She is thirty-two years old, tall, red-haired, and gorgeous. She married her husband because he was the richest guy she was dating. For the full seven years of her married life, she has been having an affair with her former colleague who is also married. She has also been in couple's therapy, regular therapy, and on Prozac. Carrie has had a whole team of professionals trying to help her solve her problems for seven long and torturous years. They have been dealing with intimacy issues, sexual dysfunction, chemical imbalances, and childhood traumas. No one has ever asked Carrie what it is that *she* wants. Everyone has asked her what the problem is. They all want to talk about the problems and look for the roots of the problem and prescribe solutions.

When Carrie first came to Mama, she was so medicated and ana-lyzed that she did not even know what she wanted. She had not thought about it in years. She got married because she was supposed to. To the man she thought would take care of her. It was never about what she *wanted.* And there is no way to train your husband and start down the highway of your desires if you have no clue what you want. With no one in the driver's seat, how is anyone ever going to get to happiness? This is why your greediness is so important to me. If I can get you to sink your teeth into your desires and never let go, I have a shot at adding to the happiness of your husband, your family, and the world.

His specialty is giving you what you want, once you've done the work of discovering what that is. He is good at producing for you. You come up with the *what,* and he will figure out the *how.* He likes activities that are concrete and can add to your happiness. You don't even need to know how you are going to get what you want. You just have to be willing to want.

Willing to want. Willing to want. To dance with your desires, no matter how extreme or extraordinary or mundane they are. The sight of a woman simply desiring, just enjoying the privilege of wanting with no pressure of attainment, sends a hormonal hook into a man, which results in his being in service to her goals for a lifetime. Living in the spirit of *Ooooohhhh.*

Darlings, Mama is asking you for a huge perspective shift. I want you to be standing at the top of the Grand Canyon, surveying the scenery with great relish, deciding which direction might be fun for you two to explore next, rather than behaving like your husband's pack mule. Thou art nobody's pack mule. Thou art my Sister and a Goddess. Your marriage does not have a prayer at creating happiness unless I can get you to tap into your desires and loft the complex union called marriage into the sky. Your desires are the connection between you and That Which Is Greater Than You. By surrendering to them, rather than to your own limitations, you have the opportunity for unprecedented happiness.

I will digress for a moment in order to allow you to catch your breath. Mama gets wonderful fan mail. It is a reward unto itself simply to have the privilege and fun of writing these books. But then my hot, hunky mailman comes (by the way, he is trained to ring my doorbell and personally hand the mail to Mama or whomever answers, and we chat and flirt for a few moments. And this is New York City. Thank you, Wendell) bearing letters of your wild exploits, your adventures in pleasure, your tips, and the fun you have let loose since going for your desires. The other day, Wendell handed me a letter on a pink piece of paper. It was from a woman who sent a quote she thought I might be interested in, from Mary Baker Eddy, the founder of the Christian Science movement. In large letters in the middle of the page, it said, "Desire is Prayer." I love this quote. See, most of you think that your desires are frivolous or unimportant. I want you to think of them as prayers. Prayers that will set you free and cut you and your husband loose to greater happiness and fulfillment than you could ever have experienced without them.

There is nothing frivolous about what you want. Desire requires that you surrender ego and offers you a chance at a happiness and union that your ego cannot even imagine. Bruce and I are surrendered to my desire as the way to throw open the doors of fun and pleasure for women and men. What this affords us is a rollickingly fun, sexy, fabulous life in which we live like millionaires, without making millions. Because of our work, we get to be together all the time and raise our daughter together, live in a big, beautiful home, have great friends, meet other celebrities and pioneers in their fields, have television appearances, get flown around the country to speak at spas and wellness centers, and inspire many artists, designers, and creative individuals to expand their dreams. Now *that* is fun. And the juice we inspire constantly feeds and expands the juice between us so that our relationship keeps getting better and better and more and more passionate. Whenever I look at Bruce, I see a man who has made not only my dreams come true, but the dreams of so many men and women. That turns me on.

If you treat your husband like your best friend, he becomes your best friend. If you treat him like an enemy, he becomes an enemy. That is how powerful you are. He does not have the ability to do that. You are the creator of the tone, the temper, the timbre, and the vibe between you. And he will respond to whatever notes you play.

Here again your Sister Goddess group can help you be his ally. When Sister Goddess Wendy was in the middle of a huge fight with her husband because he did not want to go with her to visit her family over Christmas, she locked herself in the bathroom and called everyone in her Sister Goddess marriage group from her cell phone. She had friends to call who would remind her that her pleasure was more important than her anger and that she had no *rights,* only opportunities. They calmed her down and brought her to her senses. Of course her husband went with her after she began to speak to him as if he was her friend, rather than her most hostile enemy. She would not have swung round so quickly if not for the presence of her Sister Goddess marriage group.

Let me twiddle your keys and weave you another little tale. When I met Sister Goddess Bobbie, she had been married for eighteen years to a plastic surgeon in L.A. This was her second marriage and his first. Her first husband died of a heart attack when he was in his forties, leaving her with a young child. Bobbie was thirty-five when she met her second husband. She was accompanying her sister, who had an appointment for a nose job, when she met Adam the Doctor. Bobbie looked at Adam and knew instantly that they would be married. Everyone was amazed because Adam was considered *the* catch of the year. He was young, handsome, and ambitious, and Bobbie, who was a few years older than he was, got him. They had a great time with one another and built a beautiful home in Santa Monica. A year after their marriage, they had twin boys, who were a huge source of joy in their lives. Adam's practice grew, as did his success. Bobbie was very busy with three children, and also being the primary caretaker of both her aging parents and Adam's.

In the period of one year, when the twins were fifteen, Adam's father died, Bobbie's mother died, and her father had to be placed in a nursing home. During this time, and for the previous years, during the illnesses of these dear relatives, Bobbie had run herself into the ground with caretaking. She was exhausted, depleted, and cranky. Her kids were annoyed with her, her husband seemed somewhat removed, and she was feeling extremely sorry for herself.

Without quite realizing it, Bobbie had been slowly and voluntarily starving herself. She had not paid attention to her pleasure for about three years. She was so busy that she had not even noticed the hole she was digging herself into. Every time her husband had asked if he could help, she had instantly rebuffed him. When he had asked her to take a day off now and then, she had refused. Bobbie had lost her perspective, and in so doing had jeopardized not only her health and well-being, but also the health and well-being of her family.

While Bobbie had handled her stress through blind service at the expense of herself, her husband had handled his stress very differently. He had temporarily lost his wife and best friend, so when a certain patient came to his office with mischief on her mind, he was a ripe candidate for the plucking. Rene made a habit of finding married men with time on their hands and money in the bank. She seduced Adam, who was flattered by the attention and feeling a little footloose. Adam's receptionist dropped some hints to Bobbie, who responded to this wake-up call by starting to pay close attention to how Adam spent his time, who he called, and what exactly was on those MasterCard statements. Bobbie discovered the affair, and was she ever pissed off. In a *Whose Afraid of Virginia Woolf* moment, she decided to show him who was boss. She called an ex-boyfriend in defiance and asked him to meet her for lunch. She served him a hot piece of her ass instead and started her own affair, with a huff and a puff and a "I'll show him!"

You think things had gotten complicated? Just wait. Adam hired a private detective to follow Bobbie and fired the receptionist who leaked the story. Bobbie hired her own private detective to follow Adam. She found his love letters, recorded his voice mails of

Rene demanding money, and found the lease to an apartment where Adam had been keeping Rene. Adam had copies of lust-ridden e-mails and the description of one encounter that Bobbie had with her ex at a cheap motel in New Jersey. Bobbie begged Adam to stop seeing Rene and promised to stop seeing her ex, too. They both agreed to cut out the extracurricular. A month later, on a lark, Bobbie went to see a psychic, who told her that Adam had not severed ties with Rene. The psychic offered to have a spell cast on Adam to ward off the other woman and keep her marriage alive. Bobbie was so addled by the loss of her parents and the craziness in her marriage that I think she would have visited every psychic in the Yellow Pages if someone had not recommended she come to the Sister Goddess class.

The class revived her. She began to pay attention her pleasure, which switched her perspective from the hysteria swirling around all of these events to the sanity of her happiness. She changed her focus from attack and revenge to an examination of her desires. There is breathing room in the landscape of pleasure. A perspective shift is required if one wants to create a different outcome.

Bobbie came to see Mama privately for some additional coaching. She had fully expected that I would join her on her bandwagon of condemning Adam and self-righteously proclaiming her innocence. No. No way. Not happening. I am an advocate of one thing only— women taking responsibility for themselves and their pleasure. There is no woman alive who has to be the unwitting victim of any man. Bobbie was on the very precipice of either destroying or re-creating her marriage. Mama asked her if she wanted to choose the path of pleasure with him or if she wanted to end their marriage. She chose Adam. This required a full overhaul of Bobbie's point of view. Rather than looking at herself as a poor, pathetic, betrayed victim, she had to wake up to her responsibility. It was her choice to walk away from her pleasure three years ago, when their parents grew ill. It was her choice to ignore her family, her husband, and herself. It was her choice to go for revenge with her ex when she found out about Adam's dalliance. And it was going to be her choice to grab her pleasure with both hands and decide to turn Adam back into her best friend and ally, rather than her enemy.

This is where you really get to see if you are a Sister Goddess or a wimp. And you get to see the difference between training a new boyfriend or a guy you are working on, versus a husband or long-term partner. While the principles of communication, perspective, and pleasure as priority are the same, there is a huge difference in the amount of ego one has to climb over to get to the goodies. When you are training a new boyfriend, it is very easy to be sweet, because you don't have any history of hurt or betrayal or miscommunication between you. You can easily imagine that he wants to give you everything you want, because he has not made any mistakes yet, and you have been on your best behavior, too. When you are training your husband or a man you have been living with for years, there is the potential for dozens of incidents each day that could cause you to be hurt or angry or that could diminish your enthusiasm. You may have decades of stored anger or resentment going on the tab you have been running on your mate. When you decide to go for more pleasure or more intimacy, there is no room in that game for a long bill of slings and arrows. You cannot stand anywhere near your self-righteous, I-told-you-so soapbox. You simply have to eject your historical negativity and years of research on what is wrong with him in order to lay the groundwork for going higher. You have to be on your knees before your desire to create a pleasurable marriage, and on your knees before your goal of friendship between you. You must choose pleasure over anger.

This is about like asking for triple backflip from a new gymnast. You will want to cling tightly to the earthy comfort of all of the reasons why you can't have what you want from your "untrainable" man. You will feel cozy in your protective blame raincoat as you stand in the midst of the storm. But Mama wants more for you than a little raincoat. She wants you to feel the wind at your back and Mother Nature on your side as you slide into the power of your pleasure and your desire. Your greatest power does not come from blame, nor does it come from revenge, nor does it come from criticism. Those are cheap, useless little ponchos from Kmart. Your greatest power comes from pleasure, which is an aspect of your soul guided by desire, not reason. Not logic. Not facts. Pleasure is strong, flexible, liberating, and protective at the same time. It is always available to you, like oxygen. If you surrender to it, it will guide you on a fantastic journey that will lead you to the most profound experience of the unfolding of your own soul, and it will take your man to the level of hero. We do not have many men who are heroic right now, because we do not have many women plighting their troth with their desire. Show me a woman who is passionately living her dreams and you will see a hero standing by her side. Show me a woman who is into the cheap games of revenge, blame, and I-told-you-so, and you will see by her side a man who has yet to know his potential.

Bobbie had to put aside her list of how Adam had failed her in order to create a strong foundation for moving forward with him. She had to switch her perspective and take that backflip into pleasure. Rather than looking at Adam with her searchlight on all his faults, she had to look at Adam with her searchlight on his potential and his greatness. Just as she did when she first met him. And she had to find a way to take responsibility for her part in what had happened between them. Bobbie had to take ownership of the fact that, for the last few years, she had turned her back on her pleasure, and consequently had declined the offers of fun and intimacy that Adam had made to her over the years. Bobbie had pushed him away. This tendency of hers to take care of everyone else, at the expense of herself, had always been a part of her training to be a wife and mother. She had been brought up to serve others before herself. She never questioned it. Little did she know that ignoring her pleasure would have such dire consequences in her life.

In order to put this marriage back on its feet and create the best possible outcome, Bobbie had to remember her pleasure first and foremost. She had to stay vigorously and relentlessly conscious of what it is that she wanted, what felt good to her. She had to become attuned to expanding the joy that she took from every moment of her life. She picked up her copy of *Mama Gena's School of Womanly Arts* and reviewed every exercise. She did lots of Spring Cleaning in order to clear her head. Bobbie had to loft herself to the level of pleasure in order to bring up her marriage. Rather than looking at Adam as the enemy, she had to look at him as her friend whom *she* had been temporarily ignoring. Mama, are you saying that Adam bears no blame or responsibility in his affair? No, darlings, Adam is a big boy and in total control of himself. I am saying that if your goal is to train your husband and to go higher together, it is best to avoid the blame game, and to move toward your goals instead. In this case, Bobbie wanted Adam. She wanted to create friendship and intimacy with her husband. Affixing blame and extracting punishment do not lead to pleasure with a partner. Bobbie was up for some pleasure. And yes, Bobbie and all of us as women are capable of drawing the worst out of a man *and* the best out of a man. (See Scheherazade for more explanation. She kicked ass as a man-trainer. It took her only 1,001 nights to bring out the pussycat in her murderous husband's heart, and save all the women of Persia, to boot. I told you there were always beautiful and huge consequences when a woman follows her desires.)

Since the affairs were exposed, Adam had moved from their bedroom to the guest room. Bobbie was angry about this. I encouraged her to be grateful that he was still in her house, sleeping under the same roof, and to express her gratitude for this, rather than her disapproval of his sleeping arrangement. If her goal was to get him into her bed, it would be a far quicker journey if she found a way to appreciate him for his choices, rather than disapprove of him. Appreciation and approval are essential to further training. Rather than looking at what was missing in her life and her marriage, she had to look around and see what she had—a husband who was still by her side, wonderful kids, a beautiful home, great friends, and a world of opportunity before her.

Bobbie started to flirt with Adam, slipping into his bed at night and giving him a little back rub before kissing him chastely on the cheek and retiring to her bedroom. She decided she wanted to slowly seduce Adam into making the first move of restoring their physical intimacy. She wanted to use him as a barometer to see exactly how much pleasure she was attracting. She also wanted to give him time to begin to feel safe with her, and she with him. It was more important to her to establish a foundation of friendship than to get into his bed. Within a few weeks of this new pleasure diet, Bobbie and Adam began to experience a new level of intimacy. Adam felt that Bobbie was becoming his best friend. She was willing to approve of him and appreciate him, despite his mistakes. She was the person in the world who was enjoying him the most. She seemed to relish their time together and understand and appreciate his decisions.

Within a few months, they had moved back into the same bedroom. Adam's friend Rene drifted away, as it was now Rene who was always complaining that Adam didn't spend enough time with her or give her enough money. Adam was now having an affair with Bobbie. He bought her a new bedroom set, which she had been wanting for years, so that they could make a fresh start. They planned their first vacation alone with one another in years. They started to laugh again. The fun that had drawn them toward each other twenty years ago was back, better than ever, with the beautiful, deep, added luster of all their years of adventure together.

Training your husband is the most glorious, gratifying, soul-expanding journey you can take. To become really accomplished demands a physical and spiritual flexibility to go for even more pleasure than you might choose on your own. When you are pressed into accepting more pleasure in your relationship, the consequence is a more pleasurable life for you, too. Your husband becomes an excuse for you to have more fun. He is a wonderful reason to amplify your good time as you draw him closer and bring him into your world. I would never have created this adventure called Mama Gena's School of Womanly Arts were it not for Bruce. He presses me to become more myself than I would be without him, and vice versa.

Look at what an interesting adventure Maria Shriver has created for herself on the West Coast. It seems like it took but about ten minutes for Arnold to go from the Terminator to the Gubernator. She turned him from a German bodybuilder into a Kennedy. With Maria by his side, he was able to erase everyone's doubts about his womanizing and his lack of political experience. And Maria is getting a brand-new arena in which to make an impact on the world.

I do not want you to underestimate Maria's accomplishment just because she is rich and famous. It still costs a woman the same price to get up off her high horse and approve of herself, her choices, and her man. There are many more reasons to compromise than to go for it in this world of ours. Hats off to any woman who has the ovaries to play a big game of going for her desires.

Principles of Retraining

It is far easier to train, or retrain, when you are having a pleasurable life. All of your Sister Goddess discipline must be maintained in order to keep you fluffed and puffed enough to train. The sassier you are, the higher you will take him. The crankier you are, the lower you will take him. Your pleasure and fun is your responsibility, not his. There is no possible way on earth that your life will improve if your thoughts are all about *his* need to change. The object is to find a way for *you* to get to happiness now, no matter what is happening. Once there, you can invite your guy into any delicious desire you might have.

Use the training cycle when you ask him for something.

The training cycle is a marvelous little tool to communicate a desire to your partner in such a way that he can receive it. Usually we wait until we are angry to talk, and then we list ten things that are wrong with him at once, so he cannot really hear our requests. The training cycle is as much for you as it is for him. It will force you to remember that the way you communicate is your responsibility. He is not to blame if you fail to get what you want. If a woman can change the course of history with her smile, you can get your guy to clean up after himself. His behavior is not immutable. It is not a permanent condition. It is an opportunity for you to encourage this man to be your hero while cultivating your own power as a woman. Who will lead the way, if not us? The world has seen more than its share of vengeance. It's ready for a little lovin' from a red-hot Mama.

Training cycle

1. Find your partner right. This is the most challenging step, especially if you are in a fit of pique. It is important to remind yourself that he is on your side. The more you treat him as if he's on your side, the more he becomes on your side. So, for example, you say, "Honey, I love sharing my life and my bathroom with you."

2. Give him a problem he can solve. This means one direction at a time. You know how it is when you are driving somewhere new and you get lost. Anything more than "make a right turn at the second traffic light and bear left at the stop sign" simply will not compute. Tell him everything you want him to know, but in consumable bites, one at a time. "Can you please hang your towel on the towel rack?"

3. Acknowledge him with a simple thank-you. Thank you that he heard you. Thank you that he was here to talk to. "Thank you, babe."

That's all. And be willing to run this whole cycle, from the top, maybe a dozen times in a friendly way to allow him time to retool. Hey, he was throwing his towel over the shower stall for decades; it would be unrealistic to expect him to change overnight.

For example, we have a dog, which was a gift to our daughter on her fourth birthday. When I first approached Bruce with this idea, he was emphatically against it. It was something he never considered, and he was concerned about how we could take care of a dog and find time to walk it and feed it. I persisted and brought him dog shopping. Now, two years later, Bruce loves the dog. He walks this dog and feeds this dog every day and enjoys it. Why? Three times a day, he gets to add to our happiness. Walking Princess is a short, winning cycle for him. Unlike so many aspects of life, which are not as simple, Bruce can have a brief sense of accomplishment, contribution, and success by caring for our dog. You can't count on a guys to come up with desire, but they sure are irreplaceable in the fulfillment of your desires. And for Mama, each time Bruce walks our dog, I appreciate it and consider it a tribute to my beauty and our love. (And it's one less thing for Mama to do.) In small ways and in big ways, women have improved their relationships by using their men for their pleasure and allowing them to gratify their desires. Create a hero by allowing a man to contribute to your gratification, goals, and fulfillment.

We are hardly aware of the way we ask for things. We are so much more aware of the way others ask for things from us, and we can detect instantly if we have been treated gracefully or not. There is an enormous amount of pleasure in treating people gracefully, whether or not they deserve it. The training cycle teaches you to speak unto others like a Goddess, which in turn makes you feel like one.

Communicate.

Marriages are especially vulnerable to communication breakdowns. You have your kids, your jobs, and a tendency to take each other for granted. You figure that you can skimp on putting your time and attention into your husband, because he will just be there for you since you have a contract. Or he just assumes that you are the wife, and even though you work full-time, you will handle the child care and the cooking and cleaning, like his mom did for his dad. Bruce and I partner in raising our daughter, and he will still sometimes treat caring for her as though he is doing me a personal favor, not that he is assuming one of his own responsibilities. Hey, it was very different for his father, who was his role model. And I have to stay current with him over my feelings about being away from my family as I travel and write, for I am a different kind of wife and mother than my mom was. A relationship lives or dies, depending upon the communication skills of the participants.

A relationship is a pressure cooker for communication problems because couples have a tendency to rest on their commitment rather than invest in each other daily. You may really love each other and really be perfect partners, but if your communication skills are insufficient, your relationship is cooked. I know you have felt the heavy silence of a couple at a restaurant as they sit opposite one another without speaking during the entire meal. I know you have been out with a couple that throw constant barbs at one another during the evening. You probably know people whose friends are more aware of what is happening with them than their intimate partners are. In this chapter, we will discuss new tools for communication. We will learn the impact of certain communication styles, and how we can use each other to build new skill sets.

Find his rightness.

Sister Goddess Vicki's husband, Ed, has a tendency to yell. You know, talk really loud. A lot of men seem to have this peculiar trait. Yelling is great on a trading floor. It is glorious if you are a lifeguard and someone is drowning. It's probably useful in a war as you charge at the enemy. But it is a useless, antiquated tool when dealing with a woman. It gets you nowhere that anyone wants to be, and it pisses off a woman like nothing else. Most women have hair-trigger anger anyway, so when a guy yells, it is guaranteed to make a woman want to choke him. And it will seriously reduce or eliminate his chances of getting his dick wet. You don't want to get close to somebody who is screaming, even if he's screaming at someone else.

Ay, there's the rub. You try telling this guy to shut up. You try not to get angry and it only makes you angrier. You feel yourself shriveling with each loud sound. You are mad he is doing it, and you are mad he doesn't know it is desperately offensive. You are crazed that you chose to saddle yourself with this bozo until death do you part. What is a married Sister Goddess to do?

Only one thing: step into his shoes and realize that he keeps reaching for this one tool because he thinks it's all he's got in his toolbox. Now, how useful is your knee-jerk fury in response? Fury plus fury, and you have the Middle East in your own living room.

But where do you go from there, Mama? What do you reach for instead?

I gotta tell you, darlings, this one is my purgatory and I want it to be my Valhalla. I want all men to always remember that they are dealing with a whole woman. We appreciate appreciation. We unfold and flower when we are worshiped and adored. We love praise, and we want everyone to know that everything we do or don't do is beautiful. We turn off when criticized, berated, accused, attacked, or put down. One of the most useful phrases that I teach men in my Mama Gena Gives It Up to Men course is "You are so beautiful when you are angry." There is not a woman alive who would not appreciate hearing this sentence.

And the only way for women to create nirvana is to forgo an eye for an eye and focus on appreciating him. When you hear him roar, you could say something like, "I love how passionate you are about me!" A man is successful only when the woman appreciates what he's doing truly, even if he's not doing it exactly right, and then guides him, with approval and appreciation, in a more delicious direction. The problem is not with the yeller. It is with the yell-ee. Vicki failed to appreciate Ed's yelling. When he yelled, she heard it as a personal attack. Vicki found it much easier to encourage her dog to stop barking than her husband. And it is certainly easier to graciously train someone else's husband than your own. It is a real challenge for women to love and trust ourselves enough to love and trust our men. What Ed was actually was doing when he yelled was serving Vicki and her goals in the best way he knew how. When he yelled about her tendency to be late, it was only because he wanted her to get where they were going on time. He was doing an unpleasant thing, but he was actually trying to take care of her. One day, Ed screamed like the devil on the phone to the director of their daughters' day camp when she called to remind him that the deposit was due. Rather than lunge for Ed's nuts and side with the director, who now thinks her husband is a serial killer, Vicki apologized to her and explained that Ed was in the middle of a big payment to the IRS and very nervous about their finances. She seemed to understand. Vicki had Ed drop off flowers and a note of apology to the director, so he would feel good when he saw her next. And to Ed she said, "Of course you were upset, honey. You were trying to balance the books and pay the taxes and pay the bills, and it is such a challenging thing to do. And you are doing such a good job at handling it all, and I really appreciate that you are doing it!" Which is the truth. Vicki would not want to balance the books or negotiate with the IRS or pay the taxes or bills. She is truly grateful that he handles all that. And he is getting better and better every day at taking care of all those myriad details. Vicki made the decision that she was not going to turn on him just because he had a bout of temporary insanity, induced by financial stress. She was much more interested in her happiness than in her anger.

Talk to him as if you were on his side.
It is really hard even remotely to want to be on the side of someone who is doing something that hurts our feelings or our ego. When my six-year-old daughter screams, "Mommy, I hate you!" at her bedtime, I do not take it personally. I know she is a developing girl,

learning to deal with her strong feelings and wanting to have her way. I can totally see her point. When my husband yells or forgets to bring the shopping list to the store or says no to something I want, it is much trickier to be on his side. But his side is the most pleasurable place to be. And it is the quickest way to reach my goals, which is important to a lusty gal such as myself.

When it comes to this point, I do seem to have a memory like a sieve, however. Let's just say, on a good day, I will step into his moccasins and take a look around. Our pal Oprah helped me with this one. One day she had a show that still haunts me. It was a bunch of guys talking about how the only emotion they were allowed to have as boys was anger. They were discouraged from tenderness, from sadness, from any expression of other sorts of feelings. All they got was the rage button. So sometimes when a man is feeling vulnerable or sad or overwhelmed, he will yell. The sight of these perfectly sweet guys struggling to wrap words around their feelings moved me very much. If you had had the training he has had, you would respond in the way he responds. If you can climb into the trenches with him and see the view, you both can figure out a way up.

*Appreciate his steps and accuse him of
already being the man you want him to be.*

This method works like an absolute charm, but it depends on you and your ability to plan in advance and be fluffed and happy. Guys will fulfill your expectations of them, even exceed your expectations. It's not just true of guys, it's true of everyone. If you build it, they will come. When you talk to plants, they grow better. In 1961 President

Kennedy said we would walk on the moon in ten years, and we did. Our vision has power to inspire good or evil. Sister Goddess Fran and her family were driving three hours to her parents' house for a Christmas dinner. They were stuck in traffic. Fran's husband, Steve, has frequent bouts of road rage at times like this. At first seething, Fran said, "Steve, that is so unlike you! You are usually such a calm person under stress!" Steve was speechless as he tried to readjust his perception of himself. And Fran rolled down her window and started yelling at the traffic, "Nincompoops! Oh, what fools we mortals be!" Then she launched into Christmas carols, and her children joined in. It was plain impossible for Steve to seethe under these circumstances. First, his wife told him he was actually a calm driver, and then she was being hilarious. Fun sets you free.

As a culture, we are so hooked on instant gratification that we don't understand the beauty and patience of taking baby steps in the direction of expanding our pleasure. Keep your standards high and go for everything you desire with this man while remembering that tiny steps are the fastest, most efficient pace toward your goal.

> When you ask for something you want,
> make sure it is a true desire born out
> of pleasure, not ego or revenge.

You can tell which is which by the way the request makes you feel. If you are pleasured when you ask, it is a true desire. If you are being a bully when you ask, it is ego or revenge, which will never lead to happiness.

After I wrote my first book, I had visions of success like nobody's business. I actually felt like I deserved every model of Manolo in the Blahnik shop. And I deserved first-class travel and spas and a designer-only wardrobe. After all, look what I had done for womanity! And like every woman, I did deserve all the lovely things in life, but I was insisting on them, rather than enjoying what I had and allowing the lovelies to be attracted to me, drop by drop. Bruce did his best to keep up with who I thought I was, but it was a real challenge for him financially. I dug us into some debt. I could not go on a book tour in Nine West, after all! Once I realized that authors do not, as a rule, make a vast fortune, I was quite shocked. I had expected movie star wages. Not to mention that everyone in my vicinity had to deal with my huge, self-righteous ego. Especially my sweet husband. So I did what anyone interested in more fun than I was having would do. I got over myself. And gave it up. And decided just to see how much pleasure I could have from what already surrounded me, and enjoy what I attracted, rather than concentrating on what I deserved to acquire. I did not shop for a year. But I never stopped attracting things. My pal Michele, a jeans designer, gave me a pair of hot jeans. Sister Goddess Judy gave me a free cut and highlights at her fabulous Soho salon, Devachan. My absolute favorite designer, Bryan Bradley of Tuleh, would lend me gorgeous gowns for appearances and give me outfits for book tours. I felt even richer as I noticed that I was attracting, rather than spending in a fit of ego-driven consumption. And Bruce can sleep through the night now, knowing I am not pressing him to the wall financially. The most pleasurable way to live is to trust the goddess within us that we are actually, on some level, getting exactly what we want and living our dreams.

Trust that everything you want is coming toward you. Most of us spend an enormous amount of time disapproving of what we have, rather than enjoying it. We were raised with the habit of thinking that if life were different, or if we had something different, we would be happy; of course, this never leads to happiness. Happiness comes from looking around us and deciding to be grateful, no matter what the circumstances. Gratitude is a decision that has powerful consequences. It floods one with pleasure and fills one's life with deep meaning and relevance. If you savor what you have, you get more. Savoring my life with my husband is not a skill I was raised with. It has required eternal vigilance for me to remember to savor what I have and to look at him for what he is giving me, rather than what I am missing. When I savor, there is love and juice. When I don't, there isn't.

Distinguish between true desire and ego-driven yearnings.

If you feel joyous and happy and light when you think about what you want, it is a true desire. If you feel you have to have the thing or you will *die* or *kill someone,* that is your ego talking.

True desire is all about pleasure. Pleasure is highly moral, because if an action you take would cause pain to someone else, it is no longer a pleasure. The fulfillment of a true desire will result in gratification and glory, not only for the woman but for everyone around her. The Monica Lewinsky/Bill Clinton affair had some stink to it because it was an ego-driven desire. It was not about Monica really getting her pleasure, it was about her lust for power or need to prove something.

But it was still fun to see such a marvelous example of appetite un-leashed. We have so few opportunities to enjoy this privileged sight. And even ego appetite is way, way better than no appetite or buried appetite.

And I think the trickiest bit for women is to expand their moral-ity to include themselves. We have spent so many years trying to fit into a guy's version of what a woman is that we disapprove of our outrageous lust. We think there is something wrong with us, and so we try to hide our desires, rather than living them full out. And any woman living her desire is worthy of appreciation. That is where your group of Goddesses will be useful, as we must retrain ourselves to enjoy the sight of unleashed appetite.

*Never teach him by pointing out other men
who are doing it better than he is.*
This will set you back. You all know how this feels. Enough said.

Play with his resistances.
Most women think that if their man says no to their desires, it is time to give up on whatever it is that they want. When a man says no to you, it is not time to stop. You are actually just entering the game. No is only no for now. Sister Goddess Amber had been living with Ruben for three years, and she was clear she wanted to marry him. He kept saying no. When she heard that she could continue to want what she wanted even if he said no, she did the cutest thing. Rather than talk about getting married, she would take him to department stores to register for wedding china and stemware. Or she would

take him to different places that cater weddings and ask his opinion of which he liked better. She even took him ring shopping. Finally, when his mom started to press them for a date, bing! Ruben popped the question.

The tools, the concepts of a great relationship, are as important as the language. If I can provide each of you with a way to handle your partner's resistances, then you will never be stopped by the word *no.* You will know that *no* is only *no* for now. If I can teach you how to find your partner *right* instead of *wrong,* then I can open the doors for more fun with the inevitable differences between you. If I can have you explore the concept of *perfection,* then you will never feel hopeless, no matter your circumstance, because you will always know there is some profit for you, some wonderful outcome, if you reach for it.

I know it is much more complicated to train your husband than it is to train a stranger. It is so easy to be adorable with a man, even a cranky man, whom you have not met before. Anyone can be gracious for a moment or two. There is magic in newness. But to dig down into those well-worn grooves and reach for your own graciousness and Goddessliness when your husband has declined to take the trash out for the five thousandth time can wear away at your very last nerve, and you may have the urge to snap. The stranger has offended you only once. Your husband has offended you or slighted you or hurt you so many times that this is perhaps the last straw, or on its way to being the last straw, that had such an impact on the camel's back.

As women, we don't just have disappointing experiences. We

stockpile them to use as evidence in support of our self-righteous hostility. Women have a tendency to look at every incident, every encounter with their husband as though they were gathering evidence to present in their own defense at a trial in which they are suing their husbands for harassment and discrimination. Your husband's no can feel like a personal attack rather than a bump in the highway of your desire. For example, Sister Goddess Martha from Texas had been married to Bob for ten years. They had a five-year-old son. Both were successful real estate agents, perhaps Martha even more so than Bob. When Martha took her first class with Mama, she was on the threshold of divorcing him. They had not had sex in years, and her second biggest complaint was that Bob was close-minded. Martha had begun to awaken herself to pleasure in the Sister Goddess class, but she had no idea how to bring Bob along for the ride—or even *if* she wanted to bring Bob along for the ride. She did not know where to start because they no longer communicated. They had stopped communicating in order to avoid fighting. What's a Sister Goddess to do? Mama suggested to Martha that she bring Bob to the Mama Gena Gives It Up to Men course.

In this course Mama exposes to men what women want. The guys get a guided tour of what a woman is and how best to interact with her—everything from how to kiss and touch exquisitely, to how to handle a bitch. This would be a good way for Martha to open a dialogue about pleasure, and for him to see what Martha had been up to. She said, "Mama, there is no way this man will agree to go to some course. You don't know him. He is a Texan. A real redneck." I said,

"Darling, if you decide that in advance, then where are you? Just keep an open mind. In fact, why don't you decide in advance that he wants to do what you ask? It is just that he has a longer turnaround time than you have allowed room for. Why don't you ask him to take the class a total of ten times? Make sure you are being fun and charming and adorable and considerate of him, all ten times."

Martha had never thought to proceed past Bob's first no. She usually would hear a no erupting from his lips and storm away, determined to exact revenge by withholding fun from him and having it elsewhere despite him. The idea of playing with his resistance was a whole new concept. It was a project that might be even more fun than revenge. So she went for it. She asked him sweetly. "No." She asked him flirtatiously. "No." She asked him sexily. "No." She did not care if he said no because she was having fun with asking. Sometimes she asked him twice, right in a row. When he saw she was having a hilarious time with asking, and not losing her mind when he said no, he began to have fun with her and looked forward to her invitations. By the tenth time, he could resist no longer, and he said yes. She was shocked but delighted. She had had so much fun with this game of communication that the outcome was not so weighty.

> *Do not delude yourself by thinking that anything said in anger is training.*

Anger is destructive. Period. We will deal with this in the next chapter.

Know that pleasure is a discipline.

The best possible way to make your relationship fun is to be vigilant about your own pleasure first, foremost, and always. And never assume that things should be a certain way. I mean, you probably think that you deserve seventy-five-degree, sunny weather all year round, but sometimes it rains. Be willing to think ahead. Ask yourself, How can I get the most out of my relationship with this guy? How can I make the best use of him? If you spend all of your time trying to take care of him, there is nothing for him to do for you. He will feel useless and you will become resentful. If you squash your true goals and desires in order to fit into what you think is his vision for the woman in his life, you will get a severe case of claustrophobia and then blame him for it. Remember Martha and Bob? Martha had to find a way to become a slave to her desire, not a slave to her anger or her resentment, or a slave to Bob. You are a free woman when you serve your desire first, foremost, and always. The goodies of life are to be had when both men and women become the slaves of desire, the slaves to the flame.

Let your joy be an antidote.

One day I was at the outlet mall with Bruce and Maggie. It was his birthday and we were there to buy him clothes. He was belligerent and moody because he hates to shop. Maggie was running around like a maniac, pulling things off the shelves. Like a bull in a pen, Bruce was itching to get out, snorting and stomping. I was panicking because I wanted us to have fun together as a family. The more I tried to rush and placate him, the worse it got. Bruce was yelling at everyone and I was shriveling inside. If someone had offered me some Prozac or Zoloft while Bruce was in that dressing room, I would have had a tough time declining. Talking about the problem didn't solve anything. I tried that. I began to ask Bruce if he thought he was in a bad mood because he had just come back from Florida, where he had just spent his vacation helping his mother move. That was what you call a tunnel with no cheese. He started to yell at me, but I was able to escape because the saleswoman interrupted by reporting that Maggie was removing all the socks from the sock rack.

What solved the problem? We went next door to the shoe store. While Bruce was trying on some loafers, I found a really adorable pair of shit-kicking combat boots. I put them on. Oh, what a vision: skinny legs, white shorts, and giant combat boots. They were on sale: buy one pair, get the second pair half price. I was thrilled with myself and having fun, and Bruce was laughing. Maggie found herself a pair of tiny, girl-sized high heels. She required them. We had even more fun watching her.

Are you catching on, my darlings? Fun saves the day. It saves the day, the night, the marriage—everything. Fun is a turned-on, pleasured *you*. And that, dear darlings, is going to require a renovation of your entire life. Because I guarantee you, your life right now is not determined by what pleases you. It is not determined by your desires. It is determined by your compliance to a structure that sucks the life right out of you.

When a woman is not going for what she wants or when she is dwelling in doubt, she begins to think that the guy she is with is the wrong guy for her. For many women, the central question of the relationship becomes, Is he the right one or the wrong one? instead of, What do I want that would add to my happiness, or what can this wonderful guy do for me today? In other words, is he the wrong guy for you? Or are you just using wrong thinking in the way you relate to him or to yourself when you think about him? By doubting your doubt, you can turn this viewpoint around and experiment with his rightness, and your own.

Practice tone patrol.

Are you asking in a way that inspires the best in him? Most people flat out suck at communicating. We whine. Or we demonstrate our disappointment or hostility in our voices when we are asking for something. We tend to think that if we simply say the right *words,* then we have communicated successfully. It's far more than words, Sisters. Words ain't the half of it. It is the intention behind the words. And your tone indicates your intention. For example, you can say, "Come to bed" in a way that will get his cock hard, or you can say it in a way that will make him shrivel. The trick is to take responsibility for your intention so that you are not pretending you want it hard when you are engaged in the action of making it shrivel.

I have found the best way to find out if my communications are friendly is to notice the recipient. If he responds the way I hoped he would, then I have been successful. If he does not respond well and I feel I have been sweet as lemon meringue pie, I ask my Sister Goddess girlfriends. Sometimes we can all use a little perspective so we don't delude ourselves. One day my girlfriend Anita came over to help me get ready for a book tour. While I was tossing clothes all over the room, Bruce came in and I barked some orders at him to go get me something at the drugstore. Anita turned to me and said, "Are you angry at Bruce for something?" This shocked me, as I had not been aware of my harsh tone. It made me slow down, take a deep breath, realize that I was nervous about leaving my family and taking it out on my adorable, sweet, loving husband. I apologized to him, and he was cool. I was grateful to Anita for the wake-up call.

Observe levels of responsibility in communication.

Have you ever been totally surprised by your husband's reaction to something? For example, he yells like a maniac when you were expecting a simple "okay." And then other times, he greets your instructions with great enthusiasm? It is up to you to see where he is and to talk to him, rather than expecting him to come to you. Know where *he* is when you ask for what you want. Whaddya mean, Mama? I mean that if you ask your guy to cook a dinner party for twelve, and he doesn't even know how to fry an egg, he may get pissed off at you. Not because your desire is wrong but because you are not paying attention to him and who he is. I am suggesting that you take a moment before you make a request and notice how *he* is feeling, rather than just thinking about what it is that *you* want.

Most of us walk around with our attention on ourselves, rather than considering the viewpoints of other people. If your husband is in the middle of an exciting football game, he may not respond with enthusiasm when you ask him to pick up the pizza. He may not even hear you. Sister Goddess Arielle asked her husband, Paul, to look after the kids while she went away to Vail for the weekend. He freaked out and yelled, "What! I can't do that!" This in turn made her yell even louder at him because she hadn't taken a weekend to herself in four years. What Arielle missed was that Paul got angry not because he did not want to give her the weekend off, but because he was scared he would not be able to take care of all the kids by himself. He wanted her to take her weekend, but he feared for the kids' safety in his care. It's a good idea to put your attention on your partner and empathize with him before you communicate. Once Arielle realized that Paul was just doubting himself, not trying to limit her, she was able to ask her mom to spend the weekend with Paul and the kids. There is always a way to get what you want from people, but it requires paying exquisite attention to them and their ability to respond to your desires, rather than paying exquisite attention only to yourself.

Use seduction and attraction in order to have your way.

In the man/woman game, any way you can get your way is a good way. And believe me, darlings, after fifteen years with my sweet, hardheaded guy, I have tried every which way. I have thrown things at him, yelled at him, threatened him, humiliated him, walked out on him, and given him many versions of the silent treatment. All these methods work to one degree or other, but they make a woman feel like shit, rather than like a Goddess. I want you all to feel like Goddesses. Seduction makes a woman like a Goddess. If I can seduce Bruce into coming with me to a party, we are guaranteed to have a good time. If I threaten him and he submits, we will both have a terrible time.

It goes back to fun, damn it. I hate this sometimes. When I am not having fun, I want it to be someone else's problem, not mine. But the fact is, the more responsibility that I take for the fun in our lives, the more fun we are going to have. Sister Goddess Ellen has gotten really, really good at the art of seduction with her husband and with all the men in her world. Her enjoyment of her womanhood is a tribute to her fabulous marriage.

I really don't know where to start so I'll just jump in. . . . My hubby, Charles, has been doing dishes, cleaning the cat box, massaging my feet, getting the groceries, doing the laundry, cleaning the tub, coming upstairs just to kiss me, snaking up behind me to snuggle, telling me he loves me and he's so lucky and I'm so beautiful, bringing me water and juice and wine, getting up early to make coffee for our guests while I sleep, washing my hair— it goes on and on! He is worshiping me. I was going over our finances to see about our down payment and found several investment accounts he has opened the past few years with lots of money in them, about double what I thought we had! And all with MY name on them! Can I tell you how happy pussy gets when she sees a large bank account opened for her by a loving man looking out for her future? . . .

Speaking of money, we went to Atlantic City on Saturday with my best childhood friend and her hubby, and while the boys hung out at a bar, Kelly and I gambled at Caesars, where a hand-some, fortyish Dallas man offered me $100 just to play three-card poker alongside him. I took him up on it, had a blast, and in less than an hour won $240. We had a ball flirting with him and everyone, and the man was smitten with me. When I told him I was married he was crestfallen, but I leaned over and said, "Lis-ten, sweetie, you're actually kind of lucky that I'm married, be-cause if I wasn't, you'd be in BIG trouble, starting tonight." He literally lit up and told me that I made his weekend with that statement. . . . He asked that I take his number down just in case I ever get divorced. And when we met the hubbies and showed them the cash and told them the story, they were amazed and delighted!

It is such fun to be a woman, enjoying her womanhood! I encourage you to allow seduction to be your guide no matter what you are doing—whether you are making requests of your husband or anyone else. If I can seduce my daughter into leaving for school on time, it is much more fun for us both than if I yell at her and threaten her. Seduction is an art. You have to be a genius to be a brilliant seductress.

Teach him to be your girlfriend.

What do you do when one partner desires more juicy, intimate, thor-ough communications than the other? How do you bring him into your world of the crispy details? Most men, when they hear us de-scribing a problem we are having, think it is time to jump on their white charger and rush headlong into fixing it. What they don't realize is that, for us, talking out loud about a problem is a way for us to sort it out on our own. We sometimes just want a sounding board, someone to empathize with us and tell us that they know we can handle whatever it is that is causing us stress. Sometimes I will say to Bruce, "Wanna be my good girlfriend for a moment? I have something I would just love to tell you about. It's going to be a challenge for you because I don't want you to fix this one. I just want to talk. Are you up for it?" He always says yes.

Are you beginning to see that while your goals may be the same, there are boundless differences between men and women? The art of partnership is about friendship and cultivating your ability to enjoy the ways in which you are different from each other. Marriage is not about changing him or changing you. It is about enjoying the differences, just as they are. Being amused and entertained and delighted by how astonishingly different you are from each other.

If I can get you to leap out of the passenger seat and move into the driver's seat of your man-training, you are going to be Queen of the Road on the Highway of Desire. And you are going to love your man and love your marriage. When I took a class in the history of theater, the professor talked about how the audience comes to view a play with a "willing suspension of disbelief." That is, the audience, along with the actors, will *see* things that are not there. They will see a castle when it is just a piece of painted scenery, or a dog where there is just barking in the distance. I ask you to bring your willing suspension of disbelief to the man/woman game. When you look at your husband, see a hero who wants you to have the world. Go for everything you want in your life together, not what you think you can afford or what you deserve. No matter what he says at first, give him a chance to give you everything you want. Enjoy the differences; enjoy the game of bringing him into your world.

Exercise #1: Hot, Throbbing Desire List

With your Sister Goddess gang of girlfriends, make lists, in each other's company, of things you want or experiences you want from men. Your girlfriends will be able to help you detect whether it is authentic desire versus an ego desire or a revenge desire. You will be able to detect, for one another, the ring of fun that attends a real desire, and you will also be able to encourage each other by noting where you're holding back and inspire each other to expand.

Example of an ego-driven list:

1. A six-carat yellow diamond for my first anniversary

2. The biggest house on the block

3. Two Hermès Kelly bags

Example of a fun desire list:

1. To have my husband give me a piece of jewelry, for no reason, sometime this year

2. To have my husband touch me slowly all over my body, every curve and crevice, for a really long time

3. To receive flowers, especially pale pink roses

It's not the extravagance of the desires, it's the enthusiasm or joy that floods from them that is crucial. If a woman has a sparkle in her eye when she asks for two Hermès Kelly bags, even that is not an ego desire but an authentic desire. When you read each other your lists, you will be able to see and hear which desires have that beautiful bell-like tone of real appetite and which fall flat from ego or revenge.

Exercise #2: Practice Asking for What You Want

Look over your desire list. Pick something and practice asking for it from another Sister Goddess. If you are feeling bad or wrong or weird or anything less than loud and proud about this desire, understand that those feelings will come across as you communicate with your man. And there are several ways to deal with this: You can do Spring Cleaning with a Sister Goddess girlfriend on the topic of your desire before you ask your man. If you release the emotional charge before you talk to him, your request has a better chance of landing effectively. Or you can bring your doubts into a discussion with your guy. Tell him that you are nervous. Tell him you feel uncomfortable or scared to ask him for this particular thing, but that you want to ask anyway. He will be as inspired as a knight in shining armor to put you at ease and make way for your desire. The thing you must never, never do is give up on your desire! And always know that whatever his initial response, he really, really does live to serve you and make you happy. Trust your desires.

Exercise #3: Secrets

List ten secrets you are keeping from your mate. Your first thought may be, Oh, I have no secrets! But look and see. Have you taught him the exact way you like to be greeted at the door or kissed? Or how many times a day you want him to call? Imagine how you could include him in your world and in your desires and confess to him that you want him to participate.

Exercise #4: Acknowledge Him

Acknowledge/appreciate your partner for something specific, once per day. No faking, no lip service. He can feel the difference.

Exercise #5: Celebrate Him

Write a paragraph about all the great qualities your partner has. Go into detail. Share this with your group.

Exercise #6: Ask Him

What is an outrageously fun thing you could ask your husband for? Ask him. The goal is to enjoy asking, not to attach yourself to the outcome.

Exercise #7: Use Him

Ask your husband for his advice or help on something. Notice how this makes him feel.

Exercise #8: Research Project

Mama wants to familiarize you with the quantifiable achievements of women who served their desires and took men along for the ride. Your job is to pick (or be assigned) a woman from history and write your analysis of how she did in the world of relationship. Was she a slave to her desire? Did she turn her back on her desire? How did that affect her relationship life and her whole existence? Bring your report back to your Sister Goddess girlfriends and share it with them. Pick people from show business, like Goldie Hawn. Or historical figures like Cleopatra, Queen Isabella, Margaret Sanger, Virginia Woolf, or Georgia O'Keeffe.

CHAPTER FIVE

❧

The Practice of Lust

When love and skill work together, expect a masterpiece.
—John Ruskin

See, it's all about sex. And no one tells you that. What makes a great marriage is when a woman exists in an environment that allows her to feel hot and juicy and turned on and vibrant and alive all the time. What makes a terrible marriage is when a woman feels hopeless, alone, lonely, unattractive, and ignored. Conventional marriage just sucks the hot juice right out of a gal. Any gal. I do not care how gorgeous or luscious you are. If I stuck you with the load of expectations that most wives have for themselves, the wind would get sucked out of your sails, too. Exactly how much fun is it to be solely responsible for all the tidy work, the organizational work, the obligational work, the child-rearing work, the work work, with no girlfriends by your side to make you laugh and no cute guys nearby to flirt with you? Solitary confinement is better. There is less to do.

When I was approached to write this book, my first response was, "Yuck! No way!" I felt quite queasy for several days. See, I have a great marriage, but I don't really think of myself as married. I think of myself as having a cool, sexy partnership with my guy, Bruce. We are friends, we love each other, we have a great sensual life, and we raise our child together. And yes, we had a wedding. But I don't think of myself as married. "Married" rings of trapped. Compromised. Abandoning one's dreams in deference to one's husband or children. Having substandard sex. Or no sex. No flirtation. Wifely duties. Housework. That kind of thing.

When I ask women and men why they are thirty, forty, or fifty and still not married, the answer is the same: they do not want to be trapped or limited by marriage. Currently, most marriages are not designed to be a constantly evolving experiment in pleasure, especially sensual experimentation. Why would a person want to enter an arrangement where they have *less* sex than they were having as a single person? And if you ask people why they are getting married or why they want to get married, sex is rarely, if ever, a reason for the union.

I have never had an individual or a couple come to me and say, "The reason I am getting married is that I am *so* looking forward to having married-people sex!" The motivation is more commonly children or shared benefits like health insurance or creating a home or societal expectations. Married sex is like a joke—everyone laughs with that same knowing roll of the eyes that says, "What sex?" As if they have been hoodwinked.

And honey, you *know* your Mama by now. Compromise and mediocrity are not even in the vocabulary of a Sister Goddess. Substandard sex is not acceptable, any more than a substandard meal or substandard glass of wine or substandard cup of coffee. Mama is not saying that every sex act has to be like a five-act opera at the Met, complete with costumes and live elephants. Macaroni and cheese can be a meal worth remembering when you are really in the mood and you eat it with gusto. Yo Mama wants you to bring that Sister Goddess level of attention, greediness, and relish to every single look, touch, kiss, and stroke. The way you take pleasure from your husband's easy, delicate kiss as he leaves for work in the morning can ignite a day of flirtational pleasure that can inform every action you take and linger in his memory as he goes about his business all afternoon.

Just because most married couples you know have mediocre sex lives does not mean you have to. Most people eat junk food. But junk food is not a requirement; it is an option. And Mama wants to open for you the option of having sex-stuffed marriages. Marriages of expanding pleasure and passion. Marriages in which you use each other to explore every nook and cranny of your gratification. Marriages in which the excitement of the newness in your relationship life does not end up being the hottest part of your sex life together. I want you to have a marriage in which the exploration of each other's pleasure is an ongoing journey that expands over a lifetime.

If Mama can do it, y'all can do it.

My extended Sister Goddess married community is all participating, to one degree or another, in fantastically freshly renovated marriages based on their fulfillment and pleasure. These gals are having a kick-ass time with their men. They brag to each other about their great sex. They encourage each other to reach for their dreams. And they include their husbands in every aspect of their journey toward fulfillment. Their husbands are thrilled and proud of their ability to add to their wives' happiness, and they all love the great ass they get on a regular basis. And that is what this book is about. It is about an alternative pathway to creating a union between two people that is a fresh, fun, and continually unfolding adventure of love. It's about sex. It's about creating a hot, juicy, delicious ecosystem in which women, as wives, will flourish and create happiness for their partners, children, and families.

Use Your Marriage as an Excuse to Expand Your Lust

What a luxury, really, to live in a world where the quality of one's pleasure is a priority or even a consideration. There are many countries where that is not the case. I am aware of, and grateful for, the privilege of being born in this time and in this country. I consider the pursuit of pleasure to be a huge responsibility. Especially in light of the world we live in. And there are two ways to address this responsibility. One is to open the door for others who do not have the same freedom. And the other is to live the most gorgeous, rich, devoutly pleasured life that we can create for ourselves, and to savor every drop. I think it is important to do both.

When I was thinking of marrying Bruce, I did not feel that I was very sensually accomplished. I had a suspicion that there was more to be had in bed than I had experienced. I had really only had one long-term relationship with a man, and the sensual things I read about or watched in movies were experiences that did not resemble what I had felt with my boyfriend. Just before meeting Bruce, I had taken a long hiatus from sex and dating, and now that I was back in the game, I wanted to make sure that I felt everything that life had to offer me, sensually. I somehow felt more confident and righteous about my exploration with my guy by my side.

By way of savoring every drop, I signed Bruce and myself up for whatever classes I could find that would improve our sex life and our relationship. Bruce was no picnic, no walk in the park. He was of the if-it-ain't-broke-don't-fix-it philosophy of life, and marrying a woman who had lust for lust and a passion for passion was enough for him. If it were up to him, we would both have taken golf lessons. I had other plans. When we were engaged, I heard about classes at More University in California, and I insisted we fly out there to take classes in sensuality. We moved into a sex commune for a few years. We found the Drs. Steve and Vera Bodansky, authors of *Extended Massive Orgasm,* who ultimately certified us in Extended Massive Orgasm. We bring them to New York City twice a year to teach this technique to our clients and students. Our goal was to research pleasure, and we continue to do so. Researching and teaching pleasure is a really fun activity, and it has given us a unique, alive, and loving marriage. We are adventures together. And as much as my husband enjoys golf, I promise you we would not have the marriage we have if we had taken golf lessons instead. Anyone who has ever seen a golf outfit knows there is not a drop of turn-on happening under those Bermuda shorts.

Reconfiguring the Marriage Equation

When we begin an intimate partnership with someone, we are encouraged to balance our lives to fit this approximate equation: your husband is now the source point for your juice, your fun, your energy, your glow. By serving him and pouring all your passion his way, you will make a great wife. This equation dries a woman up and breeds resentment. She has nothing feeding her soul, adding to her fire. The object is not to use your husband as your sole point of sustenance or to be the sole point of sustenance for him. It is to create a rich web of flourishing women who will constantly add their fire to yours, from which you will use your surplus to fuel your relationship.

Some people think that the only way to have a constantly renewing sense of passion is to have continual affairs. The author of a recently published book, *Against Love,* suggests that married love is simply not possible. She writes "A happy state of monogamy would be defined as a state you don't have to work at maintaining." And she maintains that the conservative institution of marriage is built upon suspicion and hard work, like schools, prisons, and factories. And she is both right and wrong. She is right in her observation that marriage, in its current structure, does not support and sustain a marvelous, unfolding sensual life that expands over time. And she is right that without that gorgeous, lush fire in our lives, we might as well be dead. But she does not know what a woman is or what a woman is capable of. Very few people do. A woman is a constantly renewing, constantly refueling source of desire. As long as her coals are stoked, as long as she is being served, as long as she is serving her joy above all other values, then she has enough passion inside to service an army. If she so desires.

Anytime Is a Good Time to Exercise Your Lust

When Sister Goddess Jackie was getting ready to move from Cincinnati to New Orleans, she thought it was time to stop paying attention to her fun and get to work. She stopped bragging in order to pack. After a week of sheer torture, she checked her e-mails and found she felt so inspired by the pleasure that her Sister Goddesses were bragging about that her mood changed instantly. All work and no play had made Jackie a dull girl. Just hearing about pleasure had given her pleasure. She decided to experiment with adding a little spice to her own life. That morning, when her husband, Jerry, offered her his special home remedy for PMS relief, she decided to accept in honor of her all her Sisters in Pleasure. She found that accepting his offer for a roll in the morning hay led to fabulous relief for her cramps and crankiness! Apparently it put a swing in his step, too, as he did all the dishes before he left for work and left her a beautiful love note on the kitchen table. Instead of facing a day of endless packing, she felt she was facing a day united in the spirit of pleasure with her husband and all of her Sisters. Cranking up her lust enabled Jackie to float through the choppy waters of moving and PMS with great ease.

Here is another brag from Sister Goddess Jackie, who is learning how to use the new equation of fueling her own juice with fun as a source point to add fun to her marriage:

Men are opening doors for me like crazy. With comments! One said, "Here you go, gorgeous," and another said, "Good morning, beautiful," and another literally groaned as I passed him. . . .

After a weekend of two different couples as houseguests, food, wine, and conversation, Jerry and I had two very different lovemaking sessions. The first was very EMO-oriented and took more than an hour, beginning with him giving me a full-body massage with cedar-sandalwood oil. All I had to do was lie back and guide him to do all the work. It was all about pussy! The second I initiated spontaneously because I was feeling so adored and loved, so safe and so turned on by him, and this one was a very different kind of desire. It centered in my chest and flowed out to pussy and the whole body from there, with lots of emotion and repeating over and over how much I love him. It was a complete surrender, the kind of ravishing I dream about. I am so happy to be indulging both kinds of desire—and I'm ready for more! When we woke up in the morning, we cuddled and he said, "You look so . . . Jackie. You are the woman for me." Pussy loved hearing that.

I feel alive and bristling with power and love and desire. Thank you, Goddess. Thank you, Mama Gena. Thank you, Sister Goddesses. Thank you, Mother Nature, for making me a woman!

A great sex life is something we all want and something we all deserve. Yo Mama has broken down the steps into easy, bite-sized pieces that are best followed in the order she has laid out for you. But any step you pick will add some fun and spice.

Steps to Unfolding a Great Sex Life

Claim, or reclaim, yourself sensually.

Each of us grew up in a world that is not very pussy-friendly. We are not taught about our sensuality. In fact, we are taught to ignore or despise it. Check out my first book, *Mama Gena's School of Womanly Arts,* for an intimate little tour of your beautiful, glorious birthright of sensuality. You know how sometimes when you go out dancing, and you hold back and lurk and watch others, but you don't give it your all? And then there are times when you go dancing and you really let it rip, give it up, shake it loose, and you and the music are one—you have a thrilling, fabulous time, and you have inspired everyone else to have even more fun.

The second approach is the one I want you to follow in bed. Be greedy, inspired, alive. Know all the moves, know what your body is capable of, know what you like. Take risks, getting yours, celebrating yourself, allowing him to enjoy you, and enjoying him. As women, most of us were not very well educated about what it is to be a woman. We grew up knowing very little about what pleasures us or what we are capable of experiencing sensually. And you know how it is, darlings. If you want to be physically fit, what do you have to do? Haul your ass to the gym a couple times a week. Or at least have a nice long walk now and then. Same thing with your sensual life. You have to do your strength training and your cardio. Learn the differences between your hamstrings and your quadriceps. The sensual equivalent of working out would be learning about every aspect of your delicious body—where and how you like to be touched. Most of us wait for a man to ignite us and lift us to heights of pleasure heretofore unknown. But isn't it far easier for a ballet dancer to lift a ballerina than, say, a couch potato? No matter how skilled a lover your husband is, he can't take you further than you are trained to go on your own.

So I encourage my Sister Goddesses to put on their researcher's caps. We must begin to explore our own bodies until we take ownership of every nook, every cranny. The idea here is to investigate yourself for two reasons: to teach your husband about your gorgeous body and to do this same kind of research and investigation on his gorgeous body. We have been given a gift of eight thousand nerve endings dedicated to our pleasure. Do not stop researching until you have ignited every one! The better you can make yourself feel, the better he will be able to make you feel, *and* the better you will be able to make him feel. For example, some of you may never have looked at your body. It is possible that your husband or your gynecologist knows more about your body, especially your pussy, than you do. If this is the case, and you are interested in owning yourself more, you might experiment with a little self-research in the privacy of your bedroom or bathroom. Set up the room as though you were going to seduce someone hot—you! Have your favorite drink, a small snack, flowers, music, and candles. Make a decision ahead of time that you are going to research your beauty, not your disapproval. Deliberately look for the beauty in your reflection in a full-length mirror. You will be amazed and overwhelmed by what you see. Use a hand mirror to look at your pussy. Part your sweet lips and enjoy the color, the silky texture. Use a little lube on your finger to touch the delicate skin and see what kind of touch and pressure you like. Linger on the good spots. The following week, light the candles, set up the drinks, and do the same research on his body. You will both enjoy gathering this kind of data!

Sister Goddess Therese said, "Self-pleasuring has been *the* key throughout this whole process. I don't think we really own our bodies until we know what makes us happy through self-pleasuring. Also, I couldn't have given my husband the tender, cherishing touch without having done it first for myself. Sometimes I sleep by myself and I have started touching myself tenderly—it is very comforting. Sometimes I go to sleep doing it and never get to self-pleasuring, and sometimes I do."

Explore what you like, by yourself.

Each of us is unique in our likes and dislikes. We have a tendency, as women, to let our husband's expectations set the tone for our sensual expectations. We don't just do this with our sensuality. Women have a tendency to let their husbands' desires come first in other aspects of their marriages. Prior to her Sister Goddess training, Sister Goddess Marsha would just say yes whenever her husband asked her if it was okay to play golf, no matter what she had hoped for or planned for that evening, and then she would grow sad or resentful of him. Now that she has a higher Pussy I.Q., she checks in with her pussy. She listens to the voice inside her to make sure that his absence will be pleasurable for her, and if it's not, she asks him not to go. The more she explores her pleasure and gets in tune with her desires, the more she is able to sense when it would be a good time for her husband to be with her and when he should be on the golf course. Does this sound selfish? It is actually generous. It means that when her husband does go to play golf, which is often, she is well taken care of in his absence and she is happy to see him when he returns home, rather than hurt or resentful.

The higher her Pussy I.Q., the higher her relationship I.Q. Because a Sister Goddess is not a victim of her marriage, but the badass of her marriage, it is important for her to be the badass of her sensuality, too. Each of you has the finest, most exquisite instrument at your fingertips, and it is time you learned to play. Mama has some great exercises for you to practice at the end of this chapter in order to raise the level of your P.I.Q.

Share that information with your partner.

It is so important not only to continually research what it is that you like, but also to keep your husband informed of whatever you discover. Here is a little jewel of research that Sister Goddess Loretta did:

> I held my first kissing-training with the hubby last night. . . . It's easy for me to give him all kind of instruction in bed, but put me

face to face with actively kissing him and I turn into an awkward thirteen-year-old! You'd be proud though. I powered through.

Loretta's commitment to research all her sensory pleasures added so much to her confidence with her husband. It made her feel comfortable enough to talk to him about her desires, which led to further love and intimacy. It is always when we go toward those spots that are challenging to articulate that the most fun erupts.

Sister Goddess Liza has been married to her husband, David, for twelve years, and they have twin ten-year-old daughters. This is her second marriage, and she is forty-five years old. Her first husband wasn't very nice to her. Now she is married a man who is kind and wealthy, and they live on a beautiful estate in Richmond, Virginia.

But Sister Goddess Liza was feeling stifled and depressed. She was listless and filled with an empty longing she could not name. When Liza was a child, she was diagnosed with a bladder disorder that lasted from age six to sixteen. The treatment was the use of a catheter, which was much too large for the bladder and urethra of a child, resulting in terrible pain in her crotch for her entire life. She submitted to sex with both her husbands without really enjoying it. She had been under the impression that she was some kind of sensual and sexual misfit and that she had to settle for a mediocre sex life with her well-meaning but insufficiently passionate husband. Her resignation to her sex life mirrored her resignation to her life itself. There was a flatness to her tone of voice, her appearance, and her manner. In her Mama 101 class, she decided that since she had tried every form of therapy without success, it was time to do a little "self-help" and give Pussy a chance. She sat her forty-five-year-old naked self in front of a mirror and looked at her pussy, as if for the first time. She was surprised it was so lovely and fresh-looking. She had not imagined it so. For the first time in her life, she experimented with self-pleasuring. This was something she had not ever done because of the pain she was used to experiencing. It was a revelation for her to create pleasure for herself, with her own hands, for her body.

When Sister Goddess Liza got into bed with her husband that night, she felt a new zing of confidence and playfulness because of her playful adventures in self-pleasuring that afternoon. There was a shift in her. Rather than looking at her husband as someone she had to submit to sensually, she looked at him as a marvelous hunk of marble that she could chisel to her liking. She had always accepted his style of kissing, which was sloppy and hard. After doing the Owner's and Operator's Course, which has a section on kissing, she held his face in her hands and told him to be very still. She began to kiss him slowly and softly, all over his cheeks, eyes, neck, ears, and lips. She gently lingered on his lips, reminding him to not move at all, just to let her kiss him. This was a huge step for Liza. She had never made an effort to teach her husband anything sensually. She had just submitted to his will and his lead in their intimate encounters. The pain she had felt as a child cut her off from her sensuality. She felt that she had no voice. It is pleasure that gives a woman access to her sensual expression. Pleasure gives us confidence, glow, and ownership. You learn about your ability to experience pleasure and you own your sensuality. A woman who owns her sensuality owns her life.

The kissing experiment led to a sweet and lovely lovemaking session with David. She had been nervous to teach him, but he really seemed to enjoy the new information. The next week she decided to go further with him. She created a special night in their bedroom with candles and music. She told him that this was the night that he was going to pleasure her. She had a tube of lubricant and small hand towels by the bedside. She laid back and spread her legs and directed him to very gently stroke her thighs, her pubic hair, and then part her lips and stroke her clitoris with the lubricant. They both had an absolutely beautiful and incredibly intimate, hot time. In twelve years of marriage, she had never allowed him to pleasure her in this way. Why? Because she had never allowed herself to learn about her own pleasure. Until Liza took ownership of her pussy and her pleasure, she had had no voice in her sensual life. Prior to her personal voyage of self-discovery, she had blamed her husband for the mediocrity of their experience. But no man can party with a woman in a coma. Liza had to perform the rescue mission on her own slumbering sensuality in order to elevate their passion. Hats off to her astonishing courage.

Now, you may have a husband who is resistant to talking. Even though you have finally been able to loosen your lips, he is still very silent. When you are in bed together, you find yourself wondering, What exactly does he like? Or, Does this feel good to him? Or you may wonder if there is something that he wants that you are not doing.

Talk about what turns you on.

Now that you are on the journey of pleasurable self-exploration, it is time to slowly but surely include your husband in the delicious and unique ways you have found to pleasure yourself. I find that talking in bed is a big challenge for women. It's much easier for a woman to part her legs than her lips. But since intimacy and fun are the goals here, we gotta getcha to talk. There is no such thing as right or wrong in bed. Any step in the direction of pleasure is pleasurable. We all knew that in high school or junior high. We would hang out on our parents' couch and kiss our boyfriends for hours at a time. It never *had* to lead to intercourse—it was just fun and scary to feel those delicious feelings start exploding in our bodies. The goal is not to have a goal. It is to simply relish the pleasure of the sensations that are you are creating for him, and he is creating for you.

Wanna know why? Because if you have a goal and you do not reach the goal, both of you will be disappointed. Sexuality is goal-oriented behavior. The goal of a sexual experience is ejaculation or pregnancy or orgasm. This is the equivalent of going to a concert and waiting expectantly for the last note of the symphony, when the symbols crash, rather than enjoying the beauty of each movement. Sensuality is different from sexuality. Sensuality is about enjoying the experience simply to enjoy the experience. There is no goal in mind except pleasure. This means you could hang out for hours in bed, just touching one another or kissing one another, and feel gratified. Not a bad way to spend an afternoon. As one Sister Goddess reports:

Saturday we had another teaching time in bed with a lot of communicating. It got very hot and wonderful. I haven't yet gotten
how to orgasm with the hand (my own or his), but the sensations
I now have in my body are wonderful and yummy.

Another Sister Goddess writes, "My husband came to bed with a
flashlight the other night so he could see pussy up close. It was sooo
cute."

Talk about the fantasies you have and experiment with them.

It's fun to look at your life as a canvas on which you can paint whatever you desire. The privilege of being born in this country, in this
age, affords us that luxurious opportunity. How about using the
freedom we were blessed with to experiment in your sex life with
your partner? Give yourself permission to talk about whatever experiences might delight you sensually and ask your husband to talk
about his. Between the two of you, you form a safe container for
any kind of experimentation. As long as whatever you want is legal,
and you are both in agreement with the adventure, go for it. Every
pleasure you take sets a pussy free somewhere in the world.

Why not have that fantasy of being tied to a bed and overtaken,
fulfilled? Just pick up a set of fur-lined handcuffs or silk ties, and you
are in business. If your fantasies tend toward the physically dangerous, such as being spanked or whipped, Mama recommends having
a code word that you establish with your husband ahead of time.
The code word means, stop all action instantly. Why a code word?

Because sometimes it's fun to have an experience where you can say, "No, no, no," but mean "Yes, yes, yes." You have your code word as your real no, so that you can stop the fantasy if and when you choose to.

Women's fantasies tend to differ from men's fantasies. Women's fantasies can be period pieces—Baroque castles with women in diaphanous gowns frolicking in the gardens with their manservants. These fantasies unfold like soap operas, with slowly unlaced bodices and swelling music. Or sometimes a woman will fantasize about an experience that turns her on in her fantasy, but would not turn her on if it were to happen in real life. An example of this might be a ravishment in which a masked stranger like Zorro comes and takes her against her will. This may be a fun fantasy, but it would be a rape in real life. So the object is not to actualize all of your fantasies. The object is to have fun sharing them with your partner, if that adds to your pleasure. You must really trust your partner in order to describe your fantasies. Take your time and go at your own pace.

Ask him what fantasies he has,
and ask him what turns him on.

You are researching pleasure, my darlings. Any information that you can gather that adds some spice to your life is a welcome addition. Your husband will add some lovely adventures to your world. Remember that men's fantasies tend to be quite different from women's fantasies. He may fantasize about a series of women who have one thing in common—they all say yes! to whatever he asks of them. The reason men fantasize so often about women saying yes is that they receive so few yeses from us in real life. He may want his fantasy to come true, but understand that you are not obligated to fulfill his fantasy unless it would turn *you* on and bring *you* pleasure. The goal of sharing fantasies is to draw closer to one another, not to create a sense of obligation for each other. Because I know Bruce so well and I know exactly what kind of body type he likes (which is not mine, by the way), I can play with him and flirt with him about his perfect fantasy woman. We have a fun little game that we play. He loves that round, WASPy look with thick ankles and Bermuda shorts and a hair band. Whenever I see a woman who fits this description, I always call his attention to her and tease him a little. That way, when I get him home later that night, I can remind him of that woman and maybe even have him close his eyes while I make up a fantasy as I stroke his body and pretend it is her touching him. He has fun, and so do I. Deep in my heart, I know that Bruce absolutely adores and cherishes me, which is what allows us to play our little game and have fun. We are so close that we trust each other with our fantasies.

Your husband may have fantasies about you. One of my Sister Goddesses had a fireman's pole installed in her bedroom so she could do a little pole dancing for her husband. I am not sure which one of them enjoys it more.

Experiment with some of the activities that your sister goddesses are bragging about.

Mama asks the Sister Goddesses to brag to each other every time they have some fun between class sessions. We had a flurry of "back-door" activity, following this inspiring e-mail:

So I missed the make-up class this weekend, but my husband gave me a very hot private lesson on Saturday night at 3:30 A.M. I woke up hot and sweaty and had to pee (remember I'm eight months pregnant) and when I returned to bed he slipped his hands around my naked body and pulled me toward him. He rubbed my belly and then my back and began to run his fingers through the hair on my pussy, which I *love*. . . . After lots of delicious and delicate rubbing he flipped me over and put it in the back door! Front door penetration is forbidden for me by my doctor so late in the pregnancy. This is just fine with me—it gives us the perfect excuse to be really dirty just before the baby arrives!

Each of us has a wonderfully vivid imagination and fabulous sensual desires. And it is inspiring to have a group of women sharing information about the pleasures they are experiencing. Hey, we like to share fashion tips, recipes, movies, books, and so on. Why not pass a little sensual information on to each other?

Experiment with scheduling sensual experiences with your husband.

Sometimes sensuality just happens. Sometimes we get much too busy with all the demands in our hectic lives to remember to grab some. It felt a little strange at first when Bruce and I would write in our calendars, "Monday, 10 A.M., date in bedroom." But soon we realized that unless we made time, we might not get to share the time we wanted with each other. You would be surprised how inspiration can strike when you set the stage.

Sometimes we desire a specific experience that requires a little forethought, a little planning. One Sister Goddess writes:

Last week I did something I've been wanting to do since I married my husband. I have desired for a long time to touch him in a cherishing/loving way—everywhere—all over his body. Not a sexual touch or even sensual but unconditional loving touch. We have had a lot of agenda on this since I'm a chiropractor and he expected adjustments and massages from the beginning. However, I had been married to someone previously to whom I had given daily massages—just to assuage his innate anger. So, needless to say, I was reluctant to get myself into the same situation. My husband has been resentful about all of this. But last Thursday evening I gave him the first massage in our marriage, and then did the all-over cherishing touch, and it has transformed our relationship. This sounds so mundane, but it is very big for me since I am generally a withholder. Undoing patterns in a relationship is profoundly interesting. Thank you all for supporting me in doing this. I will be on the call tomorrow.

One of the things that distinguishes us from other mammals is our ability to experience sensual pleasure. There are so many reasons to *not* go for your pleasure, and I know you know all of those. Invent twenty-five reasons to say yes to expanding your sensual life with your partner and share those reasons with your Sister Goddesses. Invent reasons to make the time for activities that ultimately add to your pleasurable experience with yourself and your partner. Choose to have a sex-stuffed marriage.

Teach him how to pleasure you.

Women are the rulers of the house of desire. If there is low desire, it could be because she isn't getting it the way she wants it in bed. Learning about each other sensually is a marvelous investment of your time and money. Check out *Extended Massive Orgasm,* by Drs. Steve and Vera Bodansky, for a simple way to educate each other about how to give and receive more pleasure. Sometimes it is difficult for a woman to tell her husband what pleasures her. This book will handle that for you.

Sex, at its best, is an ego-free adventure. When you are willing to be in the present moment, and touch or be touched with no agenda but to feel, you will give as good a time as you get.

You don't want to have sex when you are in a coma. If you have been stuffing your feelings or harboring internal rage at your man, then your sex life is not the problem. Review "baggage-handling" in Chapter 6.

You can also show him ways to have romance even while doing housework. For example, every time my husband does the dishes, it is a turn-on to me. Why? It is one less thing I have to do. I get to enjoy the meal without any of the work. His assistance in the kitchen is a tribute to my beauty.

A great sex life is about one thing and one thing only. A decision.

A decision that is supported by your interest and investment. It is not about chemistry or body type or age or talent. Anyone can have a great sex life, whether you are eighteen or eighty, whether you have no kids or a dozen of them. Let's just see how interested you really are . . .

Exercise 1: The Tease

As part of your Sister Goddess gathering, have everyone brag about a fun sensual encounter they had with their husband that week. For example, Sister Goddess Suzanna started a fun game with her fiancé, Gary. They decided to have a week of teasing each other and arousing each other with no consummation. Suzanna would leave little notes tucked in the bathroom mirror in the morning. Have you ever seen one of those things that has thousands of nail heads that you can leave an impression of a hand in? Gary would have it wave hello to her in the evening if she came home late, and once he left an impression of his aroused self, for her enjoyment. They both enjoyed this waiting game, and it added a lovely level of fun to their week. They enjoyed it so much, they delayed their consummation of the tease for another few days.

Exercise 2: The Touch

Ask your partner to do something to your body that you have never asked for before. I once asked Bruce to touch my forehead and eyelids and lips lightly. It felt so nice. He asked me to give him a scalp massage, which he adored. This could be anywhere from a four-minute to a four-hour activity. Describe this brag to the group.

Exercise 3: The Excuses to Go For It

Make a list of twenty-five reasons to have a sensual encounter with your husband. Post the list so you can see it, and share the list with your group. In our world, which is so work-oriented, it takes some resetting of your internal compass to go for pleasure. Here is a sample list:

1. It's raining.
2. The sun is shining.
3. It's payday.
4. I am in the mood.
5. I am not in the mood.
6. I flirted with a cute guy at the bookstore, and it turned me on.
7. I am having a good hair day.
8. I am having a bad hair day.
9. I have cramps.
10. It's Tuesday.

Exercise #4: *The Flirt*

Flirt outrageously with someone who is not your husband. Do this in a safe way. For example, choose a waiter at a restaurant when you are out with your girlfriends. See how the added juice infuses your marriage.

Exercise #5: *Video of the Week*

Watch *How to Lose a Guy in Ten Days* with Kate Hudson and Matthew McConaughey. Observe how divinely exposed our control of men actually is. This movie firmly places the reins of the relationship in the hot little hands of Kate Hudson, the girlfriend. There are some gorgeous scenes showing how helpless men actually are as we spin our webs around them. The goal of seeing this movie is to own your power. The goal of this book is to be responsible for how you use it.

Exercise #6: *The Request*

Ask a man for something you want. It could be your main squeeze or it could be just a guy you know. There was a Sister Goddess in my last class who was having a tough time getting her boyfriend to come over and see her because he was traveling a lot. When she called him to say that she had recently begun a project of expanding her own sensuality and she was now doing research on her pleasure, he was over in a flash, even making himself late for the plane he had been planning to take. Ask, ask, ask, and you shall receive, receive, receive.

Exercise #7: The Appointment

Schedule a sensual encounter with your husband. Take responsibility for getting a babysitter. Set up your bedroom with flowers and special treats. Have your lubricant, towels, and equipment near your bed. Play music and light candles. Use this time to enjoy each other without any agenda. Be happy as you lie in each other's arms and cuddle and talk. Do some research on each other or have acrobatic sex. The idea is to follow your desires without expectations. Report the results of this encounter to your group. See if deliberate, scheduled dates with each other are something that you want to build into your schedules.

CHAPTER SIX

❧

Obstacles

To love oneself is the beginning of a lifelong romance.

—Oscar Wilde

No one makes it into a marriage without a boatload of baggage. Baggage includes all the things that get in the way of a great relationship life. We all have dysfunctional childhoods or deep scars from unfulfilled relationships or past wounds that have not healed or a lack of appreciation for our own true genius and beauty. In this chapter, we will discuss how your baggage is your business. It is not your partner's responsibility to make up for your past injustices and disappointments. It is not up to your partner to heal your old wounds. It is also not up to you to make up for your partner's unfortunate past. It is up to you to pull out your piccolo and march to the drumbeat of your desires. You are going to encounter all sorts of obstacles to your good time. Mama's gonna show you how to get a handle on your baggage and check it, so you can fly unencumbered. There is a way to have your way with whatever you got going on, once you become a competent baggage handler.

It's All About You

In all of your relationships there are your personal little trigger spots. Common areas of upset include:

- Anger
- Judgment
- Body Issues
- Jealousy
- Expectations
- The Past

As these internal issues arise in you, they blur your vision and get in the way of your true desires. We are talking about situations that you *know* are not caused by your husband but that get in the way of you following your passion.

Anger

It could be that you have a flaming temper and he has a slow, take-no-prisoners burn. You can even get angry at each other's style of anger. Is there hope, Mama? Of course, darlings. But how do you communicate if rage bogs you down? I think anger between men and women is the single biggest cause of our society's staggering divorce rate. We think we have *rights* because we are married. "You have to treat me like a queen, you have to love my family, you have to . . ." whatever. A *right* is a wound waiting to happen. We don't even have a right to live. Life is a gift, and relationship is a gift that works best when we are aware of the privilege, rather than the obligation. We have jumbo-sized feelings that we sometimes do not want to own or take responsibility for. It is so much easier to blame somebody else than it is to clean up our own messes. A popular way of blaming someone is by insisting that he has to change or that he has deep emotional problems that need to be fixed; he is not a suitable mate unless you shove all his problems up his ass and he agrees to change. Thing is, you would not have any additional love or respect for him, even if he were different. The solution is for you to be able to hold two levels of awareness—you are right *and* your husband is right—simultaneously. Forcing someone else to conform to your standards does not bring happiness. Happiness comes from your expanding your ability to love yourself while you love whoever is beside you.

What Do You Do When You Fall off the Wagon?

While this whole fabulous new paradigm works and will offer you phenomenal results as you engage in the new practices, there will be days, weeks even, that you forget to boogie to the beat. It happens to the best of us.

Fifteen years ago, when I was hit by that interior-lightning bolt which said, "Mama, find yourself a man!" I was feeling the best I had felt in my whole life. I was beginning to recognize myself as a beautiful, sensual being. I had friends whom I loved. I was reconciled with my family. For the first time in my life as a woman, I was beginning to breathe an *ahhh* of relief because I had started to approve of myself and my relationship with the world. I had spent my whole life longing for this feeling. And as soon as it happened, I knew I could take on a guy.

Because I was thirty-three years old, and all my brothers and cousins were married, I felt like I had to hurry and make up for my late start. And that the guy had to come kind of *done.* He had to look right and have the right job and the right money. Bruce was on the right track, but he was not exactly as *done* as I was expecting he would be. He has a temper, you see. He was the black sheep of his family: he had not finished college and was a bit wild as a teenager. He worked for his dad, but not very hard. And I thought it was all good enough to pass. You know the inspection that happens when you bring the intended to your family. They liked his religion, they liked that he was in a family business. But that was about all. They found him rough around the edges and not well educated. He was not particularly thoughtful. He had a heart of gold, but there was so much fur, claws, and fangs that it was hard to see. He was lazy. And not very ambitious. But they were all so desperate for their spinster daughter to get married that the wedding date was set. And what was my motivation? Not love. It was an experiment. I wanted to see if I could take this guy, and by learning to love him and approve of him, turn him into my prince. I felt as mission-driven as Mother Theresa. I realized how powerful our good feelings are in relationship to men, and how powerful our doubt or negative feelings are in relationship to men.

Bruce was, and is, my grand experiment. I used all my tools on him. I used the training cycle, I found him perfect, I got into agreement with him, I found him right, I gave him winning cycles, I led him down the path of my desires. We lived in the house I wanted in the city I wanted, had the daughter I always dreamed of, had the business I conceived of and created, and had a constantly evolving sensual life.

And one day, as I was writing this book, I felt so anguished and frustrated because I felt like a fraud—maybe I had rested the whole foundation of my books and my school on a lie. I felt as if the experiment was a failure because I did not feel that vibrant love for Bruce that I had felt in the past. I had contempt for him because he was still so crusty. He ate with a shovel. He lacked the drive or discipline that certain men have. The premise of my experiment had been to take all these actions and to expect that he was going to turn into the vision of a man that I had inside my head and then, as he changed, a feeling of love would come over me. I felt like tossing this manuscript into the river.

I did what I always do when I get into trouble. I called Dr. Vera Bodansky.

She said, "Honey, stop being so hard on yourself. If you are feeling guilty about the fact that your relationship with Bruce is not thriving right now, understand that you have been pouring yourself into writing a book, raising a child, managing a household, and running a school. The shoemaker's children are always down at the heel. And you know what you could do right now? You could just grab a few minutes with him each day and talk to him and approve of him. Just five minutes."

I always do what Dr. Vera Bodansky says. As the foremost researcher and educator in the area of sensuality, she is the icon of orgasm. She is also sixty-eight and gorgeous and has a great marriage to the other icon of orgasm, Dr. Steve Bodansky.

I sat down with Bruce and we chatted about nothing and everything, and I deliberately approved of him. This turned out to be rather easy, and so much fun. It was an extraordinary experience, actually, to approve of the man that I had been standing in judgment of. I realized that there was so much to approve of. I love the way he looks, the color of his skin, his thick, shiny black hair. I love the way he smells and the way he feels. I looked around and saw more to love. He has stood by my side and loved me, while I have been playing Madame Curie with him as my experiment.

A woman's approval is the essence of her radiance. She does not wait for things to be different before she gives her approval. She approves because it is just so pleasurable to approve and to notice that, no matter what's happening, there is always something to approve of. Certainly the sun feels that way. She shines purely because she can, because it is her design. Well, it is your design, too. And mine. And it is not just an option, it is a responsibility and a pleasure, the way nature is a responsibility and a pleasure.

Finding Your Radiance

I had been giving approval to my clients and students as I coached them through with this experiment in my Pleasure Palace laboratory, and they had been producing outrageously outstanding results. The Sister Goddesses' sex lives were taking off, they were getting what they wanted from their husbands, they were happier and more free and sassy than they had ever been. I kept wondering why it was not happening to me in my relationship with Bruce.

This is why your Sister Goddess community is so key to your pleasurable expansion. For me, it was Vera who saw what I was missing. For you, it might be another woman in your group. Or it might be this book or these words right now. But we as women are all Sisters and all Goddesses. I am not immune just because I am Mama. The world of pleasure is an equal playing field. There is plenty for everyone and everyone decides how much pleasure they'll attract by how much they approve of themselves and others. Since I began to approve of Bruce for five minutes each day, our relationship has continued to blossom and flourish and expand. We are like giggling newlyweds, having fun with every aspect of each other, including our differences. Because of Bruce, I have had the privilege of experiencing my own radiance. He is my opportunity to shine like the sun.

On days when you feel great about yourself, it is a breeze to approve of your partner. It feels like second nature. There are other days when it seems like a forgotten, faraway dream. You all know how life can throw you some kooky curveballs now and then. But Mama's going to lay out some relationship tools that you all can reach for in a pinch to get yourself right back on the path. These tools kept my marriage alive for all those years while I was busy in the laboratory, experimenting with uranium.

Jealous Blasts from the Past

Maybe you had a hundred lovers or maybe he did. Maybe you found an old condom in his car when you were dating, and you have never really been able to trust him. Or when you met him, he was in love with another woman and you are not sure, even twenty years later, if he ever got over her. In fact, you are pretty sure he has not. Like a child who is afraid of the bogeyman in the dark, you can let your past, or his, grow wildly out of control and obscure whatever is happening in the present. Some couples have had their whole relationship destroyed because of a past that invaded their present.

Two training skills are necessary to keep the past from creeping up on you. One is to notice that whatever you put your attention on grows. If you think about how fat you are, then you begin to see fat everywhere on your body. You can take this powerful tool, your mind's eye, and aim it in any direction you wish. If you think about how beautiful your body looks, *that's* what you see. Sister Goddess Megan, from Phoenix, was obsessed by the thought that her handsome fashion photographer husband, Alexander, was actually in love with the woman he had been dating before he married her.

They had been married for ten years, had three lovely kids and a magnificent life together, but she would not get herself off that trail. It was causing her daily pain and anguish. Megan had once been a top fashion model, but she was still plagued by doubts.

We had to teach Megan how to shift her attention from the past to the present. So many people live in the past or the future, rather than the present. People who live in the past always experience loss, regret, and sadness. People who live in the future are in a state of worry and fear. The present moment is always pleasurable. You can always find your way to the present by doing something pleasurable for yourself, such as putting on a favorite piece of music or making a drink you love or simply looking at yourself in the mirror and giving yourself a little thumbs-up and a wink. Living in the past or the future is just a nasty little habit that diminishes your fun. If you expand your fun in the present moment, you will learn to live there. Mama had her do daily Spring Cleanings, which are a marvelous tool to get rid of whatever dust balls of negativity and unhappiness are clouding your mind. As Megan practiced living in the present, she began to notice the signs of love and devotion between her and Alexander that had been there all along. She noticed how he called her in the middle of each day, how he counted on her advice, how he appreciated the way she handled the children, how he looked at her with love in his eyes. The next step for them was to expand the pleasure they took from each other and created for each other, each and every day. Megan wanted more sensual time and attention from him. Instead of asking for that directly, she had allowed this crazy idea of the previous girlfriend to grow into a wall between them. Now that we had put that problem to bed, it was time to get her husband back into her bed. She and her husband took some classes to learn how to expand their sensual life. Now Megan is really happy, and so is Alexander.

Choose Pleasure over Anger

Can you see how pleasure is a choice? It is a choice we are not accustomed to making, but it is a choice. Jesus figured it out. He said if someone smites you on the cheek, you do not have to smite him back. You can give him your other cheek. Now, that is pretty sophisticated thinking, especially for a man. Awesome, actually. But darlings, women can do much better than that with one pinkie on a bad hair day. If someone smites us on the cheek, we do not have to smite him back: we can have him pleasure us.

Give in to Gain Control

Do you want to be able to take control of any and every circumstance in which you find yourself? To have your way, no matter how much resistance is in your path? You can, through pleasure. My husband is a master of *no*. For him, *no* is like a little island where he thinks he can remain safe from the constantly changing world in which we live. I don't want to disturb his illusion. *No* is his blankie, and we all could use a blankie. So Yo Mama has had to develop a method of having her way that does not involve being willful, forceful, overbearing, angry, dominating, and belligerent. And this method is far simpler and feels much better than going on the warpath. I just get into agreement with wherever he is. I am on his side, and I still pursue my desires. Years ago, when I taught second grade, I used this method on my class when I wanted to take control of them in a way that felt good to everyone. People usually associate taking control with force or domination; I know we have all had teachers who yelled at us or threatened us. The problem with that method is it does not leave the teacher feeling very good. You can feel exhausted and spent when you yell or threaten. To have fun with my kids and feel great, I had to get into agreement with where they were in order to accomplish my lesson plan and have everyone feel good. So, for example, if I came to class and the kids were all wound up with a bad case of spring fever, rather than force them to quiet down right away for story time, I would run them around the playground a few times to spend all that extra energy. Once they were tired out, they were only too happy to collapse and listen to a story.

This same method works on grown-ups. If you want to take control of someone and move him in your direction, first have a clear idea of where it is you want to go. Then you can simply agree with what he wants while keeping your eye on the prize. When you agree with people, they feel heard and included and they are able to loosen their grip on whatever they were fighting for. If you disagree, the tendency is for them to hold very tightly to their own viewpoint and exclude yours. I have taught this method, with great effect, to many Sister Goddesses.

Sister Goddess Kimberly had been married to Julien for three years. They lived in Boston. While they were dating, Kimberly spoke often about her desire for a beach house on Cape Cod. Julien is French, and for him, the only beach house worth having was in Nice or Cannes or St. Tropez; he considered the Cape to be bourgeois and boring. Kimberly was depressed about this for five years, until her son Pierre was born. They decided to get a weekend house outside Boston. She and Julien shopped on the Internet, and Kimberly saw an adorable house in Orleans. Her husband considered it ugly and boring and wanted a house in Chatham. So she went with him to see all the houses that he had chosen and gave them all a fair chance and expressed her enthusiasm. Then she asked the broker to drive by the house that she liked. Julien refused to get out of the car. Kimberly went in and saw immediately that *this* was her house. She went back to the car and begged Julien to have a look. He literally ran through the house, shaking his head the whole time. He spent the next week bidding on another house and wanted to go out to see it again the following weekend. Kimberly agreed, on the condition that they stop and see the house she liked, too. Julien agreed. After taking his second tour of Kimberly's house, Julien agreed that it had some potential. They lost the bid on the first house and went to see her house for the third time, and Julien made a bid on it. Three months later, they closed on Kimberly's house! After spending their first weekend there, Julien kept running over to Kimberly and grabbing her and kissing her and telling her that they had gotten the best house, that he already felt at home there and could not be happier. To celebrate, he went out and bought her Frette sheets for the bed, and a stationwagon to transport her and the baby to the beach in comfort and style. An American station-wagon was a real departure for her sexy French husband!

Kimberly got totally into agreement with Julien, allowing him to bid on the house he wanted, and she still pursued her desires. By being in agreement with him, she was able to take control of the situation, which led to everyone's happiness.

Bogeymen You Can't Control

When you make it through the problems you create for yourself, the problems created by other people will be sitting right outside your door, waiting for your dexterous attention. The more talking you do, the easier your journey will be. If you prioritize the partnership, the pathway to pleasure emerges.

Building a life as a couple and as a family is very different from building a life as a single person. Learning to make decisions as a team, rather than as individuals, was a challenge for me and for Bruce, as we had both been single for many years. I see other couples struggle with the same challenge on a daily basis. The goal of working together is not to please or cater to the other person. The goal is to add to your pleasure and to educate others how best to treat you.

Family obligations and in-laws are tricky business. They are strongly opinionated people who have expectations of you that you may or may not be interested in fulfilling. If Mama can get the two of you on the same page about how to relate to these people, we have a shot at having some fun with them. If there is derision, the in-laws will sniff it out and pounce. If there is unity, you are in control.

In addition to your husband, there are lots of people who are part of your marriage—in-laws, ex-husbands or ex-boyfriends, ex-wives or ex-girlfriends, children, and stepchildren. They can add a lot of joy or a lot of heartache to your life. The main goal here is to remember that you did not marry the Outsiders. You married your husband. And it is up to you to find a way to "step together, step touch" and dance to the same beat, despite what the Outsiders want, say, or do.

This was not the case with the following couple. Sister Goddess Shelly married Max about a year before she came to the School of Womanly Arts. They came to Mama to solve an insurmountable issue between them. This was Shelly's first marriage, and Max's second. They had had a small wedding the previous year, and no one in Max's family had attended. Max came from a Jewish family that was very religious and traditional. His first wife had been Jewish, and his family simply would not get over the divorce, nor were they interested in meeting the African American girl who was marrying their son. Shelly was deeply hurt by this. Devastated, really. She found that she was unable to summon any friendly feelings toward his family, and she was deeply hurt that Max did not seem to understand or share her upset. He kept going to family dinner at his mom's every Friday, and Shelly grew more upset and more distant from him with each passing week.

When they came to Mama, they faced some major obstacles: to make Max understand how deeply Shelly had been hurt and to persuade him to be on her side, rather than defend his family against her. When a man marries a woman, it is time for him to detach himself from the apron strings of his mother and wind himself round the pussy of his wife. Shelly had to feel she was his number one or the marriage would continue to sink. Max had been so busy defending his mama that he did not see this. It took Papa Bruce to open Max's mind. Sometimes a guy can hear a guy better than he can hear a woman. Bruce told Max he was being a dense, thoughtless mama's boy and his wife would leave him unless he immediately began to prioritize her. Once Bruce laid it out for him, Max woke up and was ready to spring into action in defense of his bride. What Shelly wanted was for Max to go to his family and explain to them that Shelly was hurt, and why. He was to get them to see how hurtful their refusal to participate in the wedding had been to Shelly and that Max's first obligation was to his wife's happiness, not to his family. He told them that until they apologized to Shelly and repaired the damage they had done, he was not going to come for Shabbat dinner.

Friday night rolled around, and Max was home with Shelly. The next day, Max's mom was on the phone to Shelly, asking if she could come visit. Tuesday came, and so did his entire family, bearing a wedding gift, flowers, and apologies. Shelly could breathe for the first time in a year. A united front is powerful.

Here's another family situation involving Sister Goddess Cathy, whose husband, Victor, and his temper are a continual challenge to her and her temper.

> Victor has been really pissing me off lately. He hates my parents and refuses to go visit them with me and our kids. All he does is criticize my parents. I think he resents how successful they are and how much I love them. This makes me so mad! All I want to do is yell at him. It's 5:30 A.M., he's snoring, and I'm up all pissed off now. It's strange—I felt fine earlier.
>
> My question is: How do you all suggest I release this anger I have toward him right now? And how do I enforce the boundary that he chooses to ignore, which says, "You may not talk to me about my family like that?"
>
> This is a perfect example of how I find it hard to man-train. I do not find this challenge cute. I do not feel satisfied saying, "You are so cute when you get angry at my parents." I want to strangle him. Any Sister Goddess suggestions? My old strategies are obviously not working.

Sister Goddess Cathy took her quandary to the e-brag group with her Sister Goddesses. They immediately saw the problem as Cathy's challenge in finding a way to appreciate and approve of her husband, Victor, while he was disapproving of her parents. It is impossible to address the Outsiders until you have it going on with the Insiders. Sister Goddess Kay wrote back to Cathy, describing the challenges she has had over the years in getting her husband, Kevin, to come to visit her family in Kentucky. This year she had the best visit ever to

Kentucky, and Kevin had the best time, too. Why? Well, Kevin had an extremely unhappy childhood. Kay kept pressuring him to approve of her family and enjoy them. But then she realized that might never happen and she should not wait for him to change. She should just go to Kentucky whenever she wanted, for herself, and not expect Kevin to feel the same way about her parents as she does. This lightened the pressure on Kevin considerably, and they had a nice visit. Kay found a way to approve of Kevin just as he was, which in turn allowed him to enjoy the family visit more than ever.

When Cathy read this e-mail, she realized she could find a way to approve of her husband, too, even though he did not feel the same way about her family as she did. In fact, as she reflected, she realized that she very often held her father up as a point of comparison for Victor, implying that Victor did not do as well as her father financially or emotionally. Cathy was the one who was standing in the way of Victor drawing closer to her family, and she was able to realize this when she read Kay's story. As a consequence, Cathy got the whole family to go to her parents' house, and everyone had a nice time. Why? Cathy was on her husband's side for the first time.

Cathy experienced a breakthrough when she stopped feeling like she had a right to have Victor behave a certain way toward her parents. She realized that he was right in his point of view, and she was right in her point of view, and both points of view could coexist, side by side. She also decided that she could approve of her husband and pursue her goals at the same time, which led him to approve of her. Disapproval leads to anger. If you can hold two levels of awareness, the path toward your goals opens.

Money

And how about money? Do you pay for everything? Or does he? Do you like to spend everything you earn, and does he like to save every penny you make? What if he takes risks with your money that you are not prepared to take? What if he "wastes" money on expensive clothes and vacations, while you are saving for a new home? Or what if the spouse with more money uses the money as a power tool to dominate his or her partner? Our culture has a tendency to make the people with cash feel more important than those people without it. If this happens in a marriage, it sets up an ugly balance of power that can doom a relationship.

I am not going to give you any financial advice. Check out the brilliant Suze Orman or the fabulous Robert Kiyosaki. I am the Pleasure Queen, not your financial adviser. But I will tell you that the happiest marriages I have seen are ones in which the couple uses their financial resources as if they were on the same team, with the same goals. Money can divide you or it can pull you closer. It is simply another tool to create intimacy; it must not be a bigger priority than your happiness or a bigger goal than your passion and friendship. These days our culture honors money above all else. If you live your marriage that way, your life becomes superficial, boring, and devoid of intimacy, passion, and meaning. To have a kick-ass romantic adventure with another human being, the couple has to worship pussy more than money. If you do that, you will make all the cash you require, besides. When Bruce and I started our school, money was never the goal. Our goal was to have a lifestyle that would allow us to live and work together, spend lots of time with each other, raise our child together, and open the doors of pleasure and fun for others. We have increased our income by about 500 percent over the last five years. When you go for pleasure, success always follows. When you go for success, your chances for pleasure are fifty-fifty. In so many marriages, money becomes the big issue. People use money as a way of not being true to their passionate dreams and desires.

Mama wants to encourage her darlings to wake up. You are never going to get to Oz if you all keep sleeping in the poppy field. Destruction of passion should be a federal offense. It's worse than littering in the Grand Canyon. Or wearing actual leopard. It's right up there with the devastation of the rain forests in Brazil or the Congo. For the world of passion is the world in which men and women flourish, and when we destroy it, even unwittingly, it is gone. We may *exist* without it, but we do not thrive. And while I am a big fan of sexual passion, that is not what I am talking about here. I am talking about passionate enthusiasm for life.

Sister Goddess Beverly had a dream. She was a tall, black-haired, green-eyed beauty who lived in California, and she always wanted to marry a wealthy guy and live in a gorgeous home in Malibu. When she was invited to a party at a large estate in Malibu, by her pal, Sister Goddess Melissa, she walked up to the front door and she said to herself, "If this man is single, I will marry him and have his children." He was, and she did. They had one fun year together—the six months of their courtship, then the engagement period that led up to their marriage. Now they have been married seven years and have two children. The hot, smoking misery between them is so thick you can smell the gunpowder. They would have been divorced long ago if it were not for the prenup, which provides Beverly with generous alimony—if she can stick it out five more years. If she leaves now, she has to get a job, and frankly, she already feels that living with Patrick is enough of a job. Whatever happened to the lofty dreams of Sister Goddess Beverly? Were they like the *Hindenburg?* Only so high and then they blow up in a ball of fire? The tight, unforgiving sausage casing of marriage and societal expectations got hold of Beverly. When she was scampering around freely, imagining she was creating her dreams and getting all of her desires met, she was adorable and Patrick adored her. As soon as she started to slip her delicate neck in the noose of what *he* wanted or what she felt she had to submit to because she was a married lady, she was in trouble, and the hydrogen was sucked out of the *Hindenburg*. What does Mama mean? Well, there was the issue of the prenup itself. Patrick wanted her to sign this thing before she married him. Beverly could feel the rage inside her at the thought of this document. In her mind, Patrick was casting doubt on their union or treating her as a servant or an employee rather than an equal. Or he was imagining the end of their love before it had even begun. She did not like feeling—as if he got to call the shots because he had the cash. And she surely did not enjoy Patrick's sign-it-or-forget-the-wedding attitude. And what did our little dreamer do? She signed. She chose to exterminate her own passion and the passion that she and Patrick shared. She walked down that aisle hating Patrick, and he never knew. And she has hated him ever since.

Is there an alternative, Mama? Was there another pathway a Sister Goddess could have trod? You betcha, sweeties. It is an uncharted pathway, but a pathway nevertheless. Sister Goddess Beverly could very simply have declined anything that did not feel particularly good to her pussy. And she could have very gently, very slowly led her man down her pathway of happiness, one small step at a time. She could have cuddled with him on their bed, held his hand, and looked into his big brown eyes, stroking his auburn hair, and said, "Let's not have a prenup, baby. Let's start our life together by trusting that we will honor each other, rather than trusting that we won't honor each other."

Instead, Beverly was handed a request from Patrick that said, "Sign this and I will make you my bride." He was, after all, a lawyer by trade. Her internal conditioning went something like this: *He is the MAN so I have to do what he says because I am pushing thirty-three and I have to get married or else I will start to lose my looks and my fertilizable eggs. And I need his money to survive, and if I don't marry him who else would want me? And I have to make him think I am cooperating with his viewpoint so I can keep him hooked.*

Patrick did not have the set of baggage. He was looking at the business side of it all. Why? He was not taught how to have a great marriage, but he was taught how to negotiate a deal, and he was good at it. He honestly was not trying to hurt or offend Beverly in any way. He was just looking at the marriage the same way he looked at any contract a client was about to enter into with another party, and he brought the same skill set to the game. Patrick's conditioning was to win at any cost and to be right. Beverly's conditioning was to submit to a man's will for her own survival. This kind of union forms a combustible and inflammable gas that destroys happiness. That gas is as invisible as carbon monoxide and just as deadly to life, liberty, and the pursuit of happiness.

Beverly did not need Patrick's money. She could support herself just fine working in book publishing. Beverly was beautiful and successful. She did not need Patrick to survive. But she thought she did because of the legacy that was passed to her by generations of women before her.

A hundred years ago, which is not a very long time, my darlings, most women did not work. Society was structured rather differently then. Our grandmothers and great-grandmothers would take care of the house and raise the children and provide sex to their husbands in exchange for food and shelter. This was the way to survive and keep a marriage and a family together. There were very few exceptions to the rule. Women were a piece of property. For the most part, women could not own their own property or have their own money, as it was all controlled by the husband. In the last hundred years, even the last fifty years, the world has changed dramatically.

Beverly did not have to become another piece of Patrick's property. She is a free woman, living in the USA in the twenty-first century. But she felt she would be a social outcast if she did not marry a wealthy guy to support her. So rather than behaving like Beverly, she ejected herself from the driver's seat and entered a state of passionless, numb resentment that destroyed her marriage and her life while perpetuating the legacy of passionless submission.

I have observed couples having the most fun when they use their money to make *her* happy. She will make sure everyone in the family gets theirs. Women are fantastically generous when they feel prioritized. When women are not prioritized, they will often take their revenge financially.

What about when she makes more than he does? Is the husband doomed to some kind of emasculating submission? No more or less than she is doomed if she makes less than he does. If the couple works as a team, then the consequences are beautiful. If money is the god they worship, there will be an imbalance of power. Sister Goddess Allison has been married to Luke for eleven years. They have relocated to Dallas, Texas; he is thirty-eight and she is forty-five. She was his boss at Colgate-Palmolive when they met ten years ago, and she was married to someone else. During the course of their love affair, Allison had to give up being married to a wealthy, powerful man and give up being the younger, cuter one. Luke is downright pretty, and he did not make nearly the salary that Allison was pulling in. Their relationship was about fun, friendship, and a passion that neither of them had ever felt before. All the other trappings fell by the wayside as their love unfolded. Allison had never felt so close to a guy, and Luke had never adored a woman as much. They kept talking and talking and found that what Luke wanted more than anything in the world was to take care of her, raise their children, and write poetry. Allison loved her demanding, high-powered job. They have created a life where Luke stays home and writes while taking care of their kids—three-year-old twin girls and a newborn baby boy. Allison was happy to return to the exciting, challenging world of work six weeks after her son was born, leaving both kids in the hands of her husband and nanny. They have created an intimacy in which each of them gets to experience an even more fantastic life because of each other and their unusual partnership. This arrangement did not happen overnight; it evolved over time with lots of talking and sharing of intimate desires. Allison thought she would never have kids because although she wanted them, she did not want to have to quit work in order to raise them, nor did she want them to be raised by a nanny. Luke had much younger brothers and sisters while growing up, and he enjoyed the rhythms of childrearing and writing poetry. Together they found a way to create a union that permitted them each the experiences they always desired.

Sister Goddess Amanda and her husband, Phil, always wanted a beach house on Long Island. They had no way to afford the down payment on such a place, as he was a painter and she was a freelance writer. But the two of them loved to drive through Bellport, looking at the homes. All the houses were extremely expensive. One day, they stopped by a small house with a hand-lettered sign, which said RENTAL taped over a FOR SALE sign. They knocked on the door. The owner, an older woman, was interested, for tax purposes, in having someone rent her house with a rent-to-buy agreement. Amanda and Phil could rent this house, with a part of the rent going straight into the down payment. They had conjured their dream!

Conjuring things is a very valuable way to create one's desires. It requires great belief in each other and is often a more fun way of acquiring your desires than paying cold hard cash.

Trust and Betrayal

And then there is the issue of trust and betrayal. Mama feels it is crucial to have complete honesty and trust in a relationship. Is it possible to create that over time? Is trust a *feeling*? How do you know if he is cheating on you, or if he is faithful to you? What if he had a little affair but promises never to do that again? Should you believe him and take him back or cut your losses and move on? And how about that little one-night stand that you had last spring? Should you tell him about it or let it go?

Sister Goddess Veronica, a gorgeous Latina of Cuban descent, was married to Stan (his third marriage) for about ten years. They were both highly successful professionals. He was a partner at a large Atlanta law firm and she was CFO of a large corporation. They both wanted the same thing: no children and the freedom to pursue their careers. They had a beautiful home in suburban Atlanta. A perfect life. Their dream fulfilled. But something was brewing inside Veronica. She wanted a baby. But she had promised Stan, so many years ago, that she would never want that. Stan had had horrible experiences with parenting three children in his acrimonious first marriage and had refused to have children in his second marriage. His experiences from his first marriage were so bad that he made Veronica promise that she would never press him to have children, and she agreed.

Now that Veronica was thirty-five, her priorities were changing. The work machine that she had been was less and less interesting to her. But she could barely admit that to herself. She felt wrong about the changes inside her. During a coaching session with Mama, I could feel something was up, something unspoken. I asked her about it, asked her if there was anything she wanted, and through choking sobs, she told me that she wanted to have a baby, but she could not even begin to ask Stan to let go of his vow of no more children. She could never ask him to upset the beautiful life he had designed for them, and she was certain he would never agree to the baby anyway.

A few months later, Veronica called and asked to have another session with just Mama. As we sat together, she told me, through a veil of tears, that on a business trip a few weeks ago, she had met an incredibly hot blond business executive named Tom, and she had had an affair with him. The sex was amazing, and she had had so much fun. Veronica was sobbing because she had never done anything like this before. She found herself to be so wrong for having taken this action. Since she loved Stan, she could not understand the driving lust inside her, and she felt like a horrible human being.

I just wanted to take Veronica up in my arms, put her in my lap, and comfort her. No one teaches a gal to handle the width, breadth, and depth of our desires. And a woman's desires are wide, breathtaking, and expansive. Bigger than both of us. And meant to be served, not stuffed away. Unlived life will get you, one way or another. I see many women who get gotten by their unlived life in the form of illness. Or resentment. In Mama's book, Veronica was doing well. She shocked herself awake by surrendering to an illicit desire. The spot that Veronica was in is very typical for a married woman. She felt completely and totally alone. She felt hopeless about her desires for a baby because she had been the one to agree, years ago, to a childless life. She did not consider that she even had the option to change her mind or that her husband would allow her to change. Not to mention the abject fear that she herself felt in relationship to her desires. It almost felt like she was out of control over what she wanted, and she was a woman who did not want to feel out of control. She just wanted the desire she had to go away and leave her alone.

Our desires scare us. Plain and simple. We spend our whole lives trying to fit into a male-created version of what a woman is, and we find no matter how hard we try, we cannot. A desire swells up inside us, and we feel like we will get swallowed by it, like a wave carrying us toward the ocean. We never get a chance to develop our sea legs in relationship to our desires because we were taught from birth not to pay attention to them, to ignore them, and to stifle them. We were taught to have our eye on what other people wanted for us—our parents, teachers, boyfriends, churches, synagogues. Then we hit puberty, and certain desires started leaping out of us while our bodies morphed into a new form. Quite terrifying, really.

So, step one with Veronica was to have her see that she was not wrong for having this one-night stand. Hey, she had spent months torturing herself about this baby thing. She was not in love with Mr. One-Night. She had used protection. In his arms she had gotten to feel herself again. She felt turned on, desirable, and desirous. She had had fun. It was an adventure in the celebration of an aspect of her womanhood that she had buried long ago—her beautiful, soul-quenching desire had been allowed out for a night.

Despite her intense guilt, the consequence of her experience led to a most magnificent outcome (as all women's desires do). Because she had gotten to feel so invincibly beautiful and exquisitely desirable in his arms, her confidence in herself rose. She felt driven to make a change in her life, awakened from her complacency. She was able to talk to her husband, Stan, about her desire for a baby. And to her great surprise her excitement was contagious—he said yes immediately! In the end, Stan was willing to do anything to make Veronica happy.

The biggest blow was that after working at it for more than a year, Veronica was unable to get pregnant. Then, after they had given up, Veronica learned she was pregnant with triplets. Now proud parents of these little treasures, they are beyond happy. And that, my dears, is the power of desire. Everything a woman wants is right.

Did you say *everything a woman wants is right,* Mama? You heard me. Even having an affair with someone to shake you awake to your true desires? Let me be clear: I am not sanctifying affairs. Any action that you take behind your partner's back is potentially deadly to your marriage. The most fun and most sacred marriages are ones in which each partner is able to reveal their total truth and be accepted for who they are and what they want. This wonderful intimacy does not happen overnight, and that is why it is impossible to apply sweeping blanket statements. Each individual must be related to on an individual basis. In general, it is best not to cheat. But if you have cheated on your partner and your goal is to create more intimacy, you still can. It is up to you and your partner to make the decision to go higher, no matter what the circumstances are, if that is the goal. Veronica never told Stan about her one-night stand, but she used the experience to become closer to him than she had ever been. A woman who knows her own power does not have to be underhanded. When Veronica learned more about her power, she no longer had the desire to cheat.

When a woman does not own her power, she is dangerous to herself and others because she may behave in ways that are less than forthright. Owning your power does not happen overnight. A woman who is interested will learn more about herself and her impact every day. If, like Veronica's, an affair is part of the learning process on the pathway to a great marriage, it is not wrong, nor is she an immoral human being. It is possible to forgive your partner and love him for who he is. Everyone has different morals. No one's morals are superior to anyone else's.

I have a different moral code than my husband. I am far more likely to bend rules than he is. Last week I borrowed my mother's car, which has a handicapped parking sticker on it. I drove Bruce mad because I pulled into a handicapped spot for a moment to see if the restaurant we wanted to go to had any tables. His moral code called that cheating. My moral code said it's cool to do because we had three hungry kids in the backseat and I wasn't going to be there long. No one's morals are superior. They both have their value, and the goal behind our morals is the same. Veronica's affair was not irresponsible. My pulling us all into the handicapped parking spot was not irresponsible. It was the relevant next step and was in service to the highest good, from my perspective. A woman has to prioritize and serve her interior divinity, as well as being conscious of exterior laws, responsibilities, and commitments. And the trick is to get the woman to approve of her own inner divinity, listen to her desires, and approve of the form that they take.

People have affairs and have done so since the dawn of time. The object here is not to condemn or to create a blanket standard operating procedure. I have worked with wonderful, loving couples who have included the ability to have sensual partners outside their marriages. This can work as long as *both* the man and the woman desire it, and as long as there is open communication and use of protection (condoms).

A turned-on woman is her own highest power, and the highest power over a man. This is *so* well known among men that they cover up women with burkas in certain countries, so the men can't see them and be distracted from their manly tasks. It is why Orthodox Jews separate the men and women in prayer. Every man in his right mind knows that a juicy woman can change his mind in a microsecond and steer him in a totally different direction than he intended. Women have no real clue about this about themselves, and the ones who do know like to play dumb and pretend it was the guy's idea to change his mind. A woman who owns this power owns her life and rules her world with graciousness and dignity and elegance.

Children

Some of you will want to live with your children and his children, or if only one of you has children, create a family with a stepparent. This means you will probably have the mother of his children or the father of yours to deal with as a kind of accessory to your marriage. There is potential pleasure in these arrangements that exists in no other relationship dynamic. Mama wants you to harvest it. The priority is to experiment with getting things your way.

Sister Goddess Joy married a wonderful guy named Thayer who had two kids from his previous marriage. She and Thayer had this fantasy that they would form this happy, idyllic union with the older kids and add a couple of kids of their own. Joy found that Tina and Marcy, Thayer's kids, were somewhat less than enthusiastic about her from the get-go. When they vacationed, she felt like an interloper. When she and Thayer had their own two daughters, Tina and Marcy became even more hostile. She found that when she insisted they do things together, no one had fun. Joy decided that rather than force herself on his older children and stir up their resentment, she would create time for Thayer to see them alone. She would make sure that Thayer and his kids got to vacation together, even if it was only for a long weekend, a few times a year. When she gave them all the room in the world to have their father to themselves, she found that they were more interested in including her. What Joy wanted was to create a great extended family. She found that *feeling* her way through each decision, rather than doing what she was *supposed* to do, or what everyone expected her to do, gave her the results she desired.

Sister Goddess Sara and her husband, Sam, had two children in three years. She and Sam had previously spent the holidays with either his family or hers. Sara knew her limitations and spoke to her husband about her reluctance to travel with young children in order to maintain the tradition. She and her husband got on the phone well in advance of the holiday season and let everyone know that they were welcome to come visit them, but Sara and Sam would not be traveling this year. Feathers were ruffled, but ultimately the families came to accept the new holiday arrangements. A united front is your best ally.

Children are a joy and a delight that many of you would not want to do without. At the same time, you do not want to teach your child that your personal pleasure and the intimacy with your partner stopped the moment they were born. The trick is to find other signals for intimacy, rather than waiting until you have a free night to be together because you never will. Schedule a date every Tuesday, for example.

The other trick is to not compare your postbaby sex life with your prebaby sex life. It is possible to use the excuse of a baby as a reason to explore each other and get to know each other in whole new ways. The goal is to keep open the lines of friendship, communication, and sex as you add the additional role of parent to your already full lives. You will really begin to appreciate the art of *scheduling* your pleasure.

After a *Newsweek* piece came out a few months ago, featuring the School of Womanly Arts as an antidote for sex-starved marriages, many couples enrolled in our courses on sensuality. We have had countless couples with kids take these classes. You can use the excuse of children as a reason to become a gourmet in the area of sensuality. Since your time is limited, why not make every stroke count!

Sensuality is an art form that can be practiced and explored and expanded for a lifetime. You can make it your goal to continually learn more and more fun ways to pleasure each other and learn about each other's body. Sex is like any instrument—you get better and better over time as you practice and pour the richness of your developing soul into your music. And just like an instrument, it is ultimately up to you to find the time to practice, even after the baby comes.

And what about old lovers lurking in the wings? Or that hot guy you meet every time you go to a business conference in San Francisco? Or your husband's secretary, who is now buying you your Christmas presents and staying late at the office to assist him? How can the two of you navigate a whole wide world of attractive men and women who could either threaten or enhance your marriage? Together, that's how. You put your heads together and tackle whatever you have on your plate, not as a problem, but as an opportunity to expand your fun. If you love to flirt, it is up to you to figure out how to reassure your husband so he feels included in your fun. If he loves to flirt, you may want to include yourself in his flirtations, rather than be excluded yourself. Sister Goddess Maxine, married to a hot producer, would go up to his adoring pool of fans and actresses at parties and say, "He is so much fun to flirt with, isn't he?" Just to make her mark and have some fun.

Look, darlings, it's the obstacles that we encounter that give value and color and richness to our lives. You don't want a problem-free life with your husband. It simply wouldn't be interesting. You want a life that gives you an opportunity to draw closer to him because of the challenges you face together. Got it, my divine navigatrixes? We hacketh our way through the brambles together and have something far more valuable on the end, because of the journey.

Exercise #1: Spring Cleaning of Your Obstacles

Choose from the following categories: children, the baby, stepchildren, ex-husband, ex-girlfriend, in-laws, parents, or any obstacles you notice in your life. We have all been conditioned to think children and family life are supposed to be a wonderful, life-enhancing, rosy experiences. We feel awful when we have the passing sensation of hating our kids or our families. We feel uncomfortable if we feel jealous of our husband's ex or stepchildren. This exercise will give you all a safe spot to vent and spew your fumes. Do ten minutes per day of Spring Cleaning until the negative feelings diminish.

Exercise #2: Sneaking Around

Make a decision that one of you is going to plan a hot, sexy encounter at the Hotel Lust (your bedroom) today. That person will decide when and where and what transpires. Whether the babysitter is in the next room or your kid is napping, you have to go to the Hotel for a quickie.

Exercise #3: The Year in Holidays

After appropriately pussifying the room (candles, flowers, music, wine, etc.), sit down with your husband and a large calendar. Ask him exactly which of the holidays he would like to spend:

a) alone with you

b) with his family

c) with your family

d) other

Then share your ideas with him. The object here is to make this communication and exchange of ideas as fun as possible, and to remember that each of you is on the same side. Do not care a fig if each of your holiday plans are in direct opposition. Just mark off his with a yellow Hi-Liter, and yours with pink. The goal of this interchange is not to resolve the conflicts. It is to lay out the project and have fun while you examine it. After you get it on paper, put the paper away to bring to your next Sister Goddess gathering. Then reward your-self and your husband with some pleasure, like a foot massage or a back massage or a genital massage. (You know how Yo Mama favors the genital massage.) The idea is to enjoy starting a conversation about how to work even better as a team. It is a significant baby step toward your goal. Your next conversation can be even more fun, if fun is your goal.

Exercise #4: Video of the Week

Watch *Rebecca* with Laurence Olivier. What a movie! Watch how the gorgeous Joan Fontaine almost destroys her happiness as she is haunted by the ghosts of her husband's past. Are they real or imagined?

Epilogue:
Keeping True to Your Vision

A woman is a force of nature, not a creature of service. And, panic ye not, a force of nature provides a lot of service in the world. But service alone is not our raison d'être.

How do you explore the force of nature that you are? Say yes to your desires, no matter how odd they seem. Sister Goddess Eve divorced her husband, Anthony, eight years ago, when her kids had graduated from college. She and Anthony would see each other only occasionally, and uncomfortably, on holidays. Neither had remarried, and while Eve dated, Anthony never socialized much. Eve had felt restricted and repressed with Anthony, and now she was ready to spread her wings. She was living in Providence, dating again, and one day Anthony came to town and took her out for lunch. She practiced flirting with him and surprised herself by having a lovely time. Eve had just put down a deposit on an apartment that was part of a commune in Oregon. Anthony thought she was crazy, but this time she was able to laugh at his fuddy-duddy ways rather than take them personally and have them restrict her forward motion. He found her fascinating. At the ripe young age of sixty, Eve joined the commune. Over the course of the next two years, Anthony, her biggest critic and greatest ally, would go out to the commune and visit her. They had so much fun that he came more and more often, and he finally moved in with her. She doesn't want to marry him again because she thinks it is sexier to be his mistress. The entire family is happily spending holidays together for the first time in years. Eve spent her life trying to fit in to Anthony's world, which never provided happiness for her or her family. Once she charted her own course, there was room on board for everyone.

Sister Goddess Helen moved with her boyfriend from Michigan to New York City, to be with her Sister Goddess community. She and her boyfriend include other sex partners on occasion, just to spice things up. They have a great relationship, and he feels so proud of her for being such an adventuress. Most women think their guy would never agree to an arrangement that included such sexual variety for her and such monogamy for him. There is always a way to have everything you want. Sister Goddess Bridget, from Hawaii, asked her boyfriend of five years to move out for a few months, just so she could sow some wild oats before they made the decision to get married and have children. They have never gotten along better or been more intimate, and she has never appreciated him more. The frozen state of their relationship has thawed into something hotter and juicier. He gets to be with Bridget, instead of with Bridget's expectations of what a relationship is.

Life, relationships, intimacy, and love are all far more interesting than we currently experience them and consider them to be. Each of us is as exquisitely different and exquisitely similar as a snowflake or a leaf. The fun is not in jamming everyone into the same mold. The fun is in exploring the differences—the differences between a man and a woman, and the differences between the unfolding adventure of each woman's desire.

About a year ago, a woman in her late seventies took my class. She was an interesting combination of shy and fiery. She was outwardly very quiet and repressed, but you could see her sparkle lurking just beneath the surface. She was marvelously attractive and looked much younger than her years, even though she was obviously stressed and worn out. Eleanor had been married for forty-nine years and had two grown children and six grandchildren. Her husband had been very sick for the last ten years, and she had been his full-time support system, in addition to working three days a week at a day care center. All of her life was about looking after other people. She went from work to the nursing home to see her husband. Buried inside was a beautiful woman who loved to dance, flirt, go to parties, travel, explore new adventures, and meet new people. She had forgotten about this radiant side of herself in all the years of being weighted down by her obligations.

During the Mama 101 class, Eleanor was very quiet, as she felt she was older than most of the women by at least ten, twenty, thirty, forty, or fifty years, which was true. But she began to realize that we are all Sisters, and she had as much to offer them as they had to offer her. During the course, I encourage the participants to put together a pleasure basket. This is a basket of sensual goodies that they can keep by their bedside for use alone or with a partner. Eleanor decided to join a group of Sister Goddesses as they took a field trip to Eve's Garden, a local, female-friendly shop that sells sex toys. It was her first time going to such a place, and she made a purchase. She had not even considered her sensual pleasure in a couple of decades, and this was a start. Eleanor completed the course, skeptical and yet somehow altered. She began to say yes to other offers outside of work and visiting her husband in the nursing home. She started folk dancing with a ninety-year-old man who was married to a friend of hers. A neighbor invited her to her weekly Friday night dinner party. She started to go out to movies once in a while with other single women in her building. She began to have a life.

This was actually her second marriage. Her first marriage had been to her high school sweetheart, Bernie. They had married right after World War II, when she was twenty years old. Bernie, husband #1, had been very controlling and, although they loved each other, they fought a lot. The marriage collapsed when they lost their first child, soon after its birth. He went off and married twice more, and she, of course, married again. But they always kept in touch. Somehow Bernie always found her, called her now and then, and checked in on her. They went on to live very separate lives, to have children and families of their own. But you can never stop sharing the past that you had with someone. They had been young together, they grew up together, his mother had taught her to make brisket and to fold towels in thirds. That would never go away.

Fifty-six years after their divorce, Bernie's third wife grew ill and died. He was devastated, as the marriage had been wonderful, and his wife was quite a bit younger than he. He called Eleanor, and they went out to dinner together. They had a lot in common; both were suffering the loss of their spouse. Hers was still alive, but he was in a nursing home, his mind was enfeebled, and he was no longer really there. They began to get together each week for dinner. They talked on the phone. They e-mailed. And a wonderful thing occurred: they fell in love again. It shocked them both and scared them. How could he, after being so in love with his third wife, fall so quickly into this new passion? And for her, it was even stickier: how could she, with her husband in a nursing home, have a new relationship? Was it cheating on your husband if he was no longer cognizant? And what would she tell her children? And grandchildren? Bernie wrote her a poem, declaring his love. No one had ever written a love poem to her before. Nor had he ever been moved to write poetry. But there are some emotions that prose just cannot contain. Here is a fragment:

> *It was never my intent to find someone new*
> *But then from nowhere, I rediscovered you*
>
> *Fate no doubt discovered, we were owed a second chance*
> *And forward I look my darling, we have yet to finish our dance.*

And then he wrote a letter to all of his friends and family, telling them about what was happening. He suggested to Eleanor that she use the letter, too, if words failed her. They both were able to communicate the awkward good fortune of their rediscovery of each other and share their joy with everyone in a way that permitted others to be happy for them.

Society, religion, and prevailing culture would have a lot to say about these two people. How could this man begin to find love again so quickly after the death of his beloved wife? Should he not take a year to mourn? And worse still, how could this woman, with her husband in a nursing home, carry on with another man? Was that not breaking the laws of matrimony? The Ten Commandments? The Hammurabic Code? Could be.

And it could also be that there is a morality even higher than those rules and regulations we have been encouraged to adopt: *pleasure* is actually the highest moral code we have. When something is pleasurable, it takes care of everyone. Pain does not, suffering does not, even though those two disciplines are much more popular in our culture. Let's follow this through: is Bernie's departed wife being dishonored by this union? I think not. She actually wanted him to find a new companion. His grown children and grandchildren might be struggling to keep up with him, but they all can manage.

As for Eleanor, she had been living in a functioning coma for years as she shuttled herself from work to the nursing home. She was on antidepressants and all sorts of medication to keep her going and to ease her despair. She had nothing to look forward to except the occasional visit from a grandchild. She now has a shot at happiness. She has someone who calls her in the morning to see if she is alive. Someone e-mails her a poem a day. Takes her to dinner. Listens to her. Teases her. Makes her feel beautiful and desirable. Laughs with her, cries with her. And she still goes to the nursing home each day. Her infirm husband does not even recognize her sometimes. If anything, this experience has renewed her efforts to make sure he is taken care of. She is not visiting him as just another responsibility that is draining the life out of her; she is visiting him out of the overflowing joy and happiness she is now experiencing. If she were to pass on this opportunity because of what our society would say, how could she live with herself? Would she ever get such a chance at happiness again? At age seventy-nine, I think not.

Transformative, soul-stirring, ecstatic relationships come from the inclusion of every part of what a woman is. If we can go on the adventure of finding ourselves right and our desires right, instead of thinking that what we want is some weird pathology or problem, we have a much better shot at creating exciting, pleasure-filled partnerships in our lifetime.

It is a great privilege to be a woman. I feel the depth of this privilege every day of my life. I do not take a single day for granted, a single moment for granted. Because of my marriage to Bruce, I have become the woman I was destined to be, and he has become a hero. There is a magic created in the union of a man and a woman that is greater than the power of each of them on their own. I could never have created this school, written these books, or forged these pathways without him. He runs the office and handles the business while I get to do the things I adore, such as writing and teaching. He is a man who has devoted his life to the women he loves—me, our daughter, Maggie, our moms, and all the women who work with us. I know that I would not have the incredible love affair that I have with him if it were not for the Sister Goddess community around me, and I know that I would not have the Sister Goddess community around me if it were not for him. A woman's desires have the power to elevate everyone in her world. The union of a man and a woman creates an alchemical consequence, which is greater than either of these two elements on their own.

Acknowledgments

To Bruce, my hot husband. The greatest accomplishment of my life is our friendship and devotion.

To Maggie Rose, with thanks for your bossy insistence that we always have fun.

To my Mama and best friend, Bebe. Thank you for the wonderful privilege of being your daughter.

To my sweet Dad, with thanks for all the questions you planted in me.

With deep gratitude to my brother, Richie, who has loved me and supported my dreams our whole lives. To my Aunt Libby, Aunt Gertrude, and Aunt Tess, where I first learned about the fun of Sisterhood.

Thank you, Marcelo and Michele Sandoval, for your great marriage and our fabulous friendship. Once more, to the beach, dear friends!

To (Mrs.) Joanne LaMarca, thank you for our years of friendship, love of television, and for making me a star.

To Steve and my shining star, Vera, with daily thanks for your beautiful union.

To Elizabeth Hayes, my gorgeous, vivacious, inspired publicist, for whom this book is written. Thank you for sending me back in the ring for another round.

To Amanda Murray, my incisive, sexy, genius editor. My love affair with your mind increases with each collaboration.

To Jen Gates, my agent: I am so honored, grateful, and thrilled with our partnership. You have provided support, encouragement, and inspiration in ways that far exceed anything I could have dreamed of or deserved.

With abounding gratitude to Emily Remes, for her incredible beauty, generosity, and attention.

With thanks to Elizabeth Kugler, my copy editor, and Mara Lurie, the production editor.

Special thanks to Christina Richardson, for rounding third and running to home plate for our team.

Thank you, Lori Genes, for living with gusto, and for all your generous assistance.

To Deborah Lack Daniels, our latest Hot Mama, with deep appreciation for your dedication, spirit, and talent.

To Dame Lori Sutherland, for the laughs, another opening, another show, and for your exquisite beauty, love, and brilliance at every turn.

To Elvira Ryder, our Caribbean tidal wave, for your magnificent vision.

To Kadidja Yansane, thank you for going on the adventure of living your desires, which jettisoned you to the Pleasure Palace.

To Abigail Sandler, thank you for your incredible contribution to the Pussy Palace.

To Marti, Rozi, and Carmen, with thanks for your devotion and assistance to my family.

To Wilma Harris, thank you for being my other mother. I love you.

To Roberto Lugo, my hair and makeup stylist (every woman's fantasy), for your profound attention, with deep gratitude for always insuring that I am as gorgeous as possible for every appearance.

To Bryan Bradley and Amanda Brooks of Tuleh, for the dazzling, magical clothes, and for your constant creative inspiration.

Thank you, Frank Veronsky, my photographer, for the fun we have together and the fantastic, gorgeous book cover!

To Sonia Nikki, my stylist, for your exquisite sense of style, with deep thanks.

To David Rosenthal, thank you for your genius and plain, raw sex appeal.

To Katie Couric, with deep thanks for the doors you have opened for me and so many people, with your creative, investigative mind.

To Conan O'Brien, the man who gave me my first opportunity to appear on national TV, and then had me again and again and again and again and again. Thanks for our delicious, on-screen flirtation.

Thank you, Andrew Fisher, my trainer, for my ever-so-hot body.

To Al Hoffman, with gratitude, for your generosity and love, and for your talent at squeezing fun out of every circumstance.

To the man with the gorgeous jewels, Rob Eigen, of Michael Eigen Jewelers. Thanks for making me, and so many women, sparkle!

Thank you, Sheila Yen, from the Bahari Group, for the gorgeous cover gown.

Special thanks to the amazing group of women who were part of my first Marriage Class!

ABOUT THE AUTHOR

Regena (derived from "queen" in Latin) **Thomashauer** has spent her lifetime ascending to her rightful place on a throne that she envisioned and her husband constructed for her. The author of *Mama Gena's School of Womanly Arts* and *Mama Gena's Owner's and Operator's Guide to Men,* she has appeared on the *Today* show, *Late Night with Conan O'Brien,* and numerous other programs. She lives in Manhattan with her husband and daughter.

To learn more about Mama Gena, please visit www.mamagenas. com.